PRENZLAUER BERG

Rosenthaler Str.

Torstr.

26

U

27

U

Münzstr.

Hackescher Markt

Frankfurter Allee

S

Alexanderplatz

Karl-Liebknecht-Str.

DB S U
Bahnhof
Alexanderplatz

25

DDR-Museum

24

Fernsehturm

Alexanderstr.

Berliner Dom

23

Spandauer Str.

Marx-Engels-Forum

Grunerstr.

18

Rotes Rathaus

Schlossplatz

U

19

Breite Str.

Stralauer Str.

Mühlendamm

SPREE

S U

3

Märkisches Museum

Zille

U

Annenstr.

U

Heinrich-Heine-Str.

U

4

Death strip

Rear Wall

Course of the Wall

KREUZBERG

Border Crossing Point
Heinrich-Heine-Str.

E

F

Baris 0173621 38 23

2

ORIENTATION After the end of the Second World War in 1945, the victors divided Berlin into four occupation zones. Due to the erection of the Wall, the city became probably one of the most famous symbols of the Cold War. Here, two systems clashed with each other, frequently provoking spectacular confrontations. The remnants of the past are difficult to find in the reunited capital, but still exist in all city districts and the surrounding countryside. The PAST FINDER© takes you to the "sights" of the past with its easy-to-use guidance system.

HOW TO USE THE PAST FINDER©

Colour-coded bars take you to the respective maps for the area specified in the bar. On the map, the numbered items in the text part are placed in the respective reference grid. The individual description of a building or site first explains its importance during the Nazi period, then its current function.

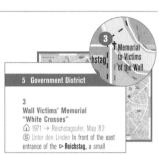

5 Government District

3
Wall Victims' Memorial
"White Crosses"
⌂ 1971 → Reichstagsufer, Map B2
Ⓢ Unter den Linden **In front of the east entrance of the ▷ Reichstag, a small**

LEGEND
⌂ Architect and year of construction
→ Address and grid reference on the map of the same color
Ⓢ Nearest S-Bahn station (urban
Ⓤ rail system) or U-Bahn station (underground / subway system)
⏲ Opening times
▷ Reference to index

German ranks and titles are explained in the glossary on page 92.

10 Crumbling remains of the Wall at Niederkirchnerstrasse by the Martin Gropius building

HOW TO GET AROUND BERLIN
It's best to use the excellent public transport system of the BVG or hire a bike to explore the reunited capital.

Tourist Information
→ Brandenburg Gate, Southern Wing
⏲ Mon–Sat 9.30–18.00
→ Budapester Straße, Europa Center
⏲ Mon–Sun 8.00–22.00
→ Television Tower, Panoramastraße
⏲ Mon–Sun 9.30–18.00
→ Tegel Airport, Haupthalle / Main Hall
⏲ Mon–Sun 5.00–22.30

Berlin Transport Authority (BVG)
Information on subway (U-Bahn), city train (S-Bahn), tram and bus routes and times are available at every station or stop. Timetables, issued free of charge, and information can be obtained at all regional and long-distance train stations. Tickets can be bought at ticket machines on all platforms or at the counters.

Bikes for Hire from the Deutsche Bahn (DB / German Railroad)
This is what you do: find a bike painted silver and red with a DB logo, phone the number stated, pay by credit card, enter PIN and pedal off.

Velo Taxi
Simply flag down one of the streamlined ikshas, climb in and enjoy the ride.

PAST FINDER BERLIN

by Maik Kopleck,
translated by Irene Grote

CH. LINKS VERLAG, BERLIN

Military parades for the SED leadership on the 40th anniversary of the GDR in East Berlin, 1989.

GOVERNMENT DISTRICT In 1945, wide parts of the historic heart of Berlin were destroyed. In the middle of this desolate destruction, the first postwar construction to appear was the Soviet War Memorial at Tiergarten, a symbol of victory. On 17 June 1953, the people of East Berlin rose up against the regime of the GDR. The uprising was brutally repressed with tanks. In 1961, the GDR erected the Berlin Wall, which divided the city for decades to come. After the peaceful revolution of 1989, the Wall's traces were speedily removed in the Government District of the City and are now hard to find.

1
Soviet War Memorial
Tiergarten
⌂ Lev Kerbel, Vladimir Zigal, Nikolai Sergijevski, 1945 → Straße des 17. Juni, Map B2 Ⓢ Unter den Linden In front of the ruins of the Reichstag building, the first Soviet war memorial in Berlin was built in November 1945. The victors used the granite slabs from Hitler's demolished New Reich Chancellery for its construction. A triumphant soldier high on a colonnade forms the center of the memorial. 2,500 Red Army soldiers rest in tombs in the back of the park. Two T34 tanks, which reached Berlin in April 1945, flank the memorial, along with two shooting batteries, which announced the end of the battle for the capital of the German Reich. During the Cold War, the memorial was situated in the British occupation zone and was the object of quarrels between East and West. In November 1970, one of the Soviet soldiers who guarded the grounds around the clock until 22 December 1990 was assassinated.

2
Reichstag
⌂ Paul Wallot, 1894, Sir Norman Foster 1999 → Platz der Republik 1, Map B2 Ⓢ Unter den Linden ⏲ Mon–Sun 8–22 Paul Wallot constructed the Reichstag in 1894 as a representative building for the parliament. The huge iron dome defined its monumental architecture. The burning of the Reichstag in 1933, the World War II bombing raids, but above all the merciless final battle for Berlin severely damaged the building. On 9 September 1948, during the Soviet blockade, nearly 300,000 Berlin citizens gathered in front of the Reichstag. Mayor Ernst Reuter appealed dramatically to the world community not to abandon Berlin. From directly behind the east entrance, the Wall to East Berlin ran since 1961. The repaired building served as exhibition hall until 1989. Reconstruction workers in the 1990s found wall markings by Soviet soldiers who had eternalized themselves after storming the Reichstag in 1945. This "graffiti" has been preserved and is still visible today.

In 1995, in a spectacular action, the artist couple Christo and Jeanne-Claude wrapped the huge building in a plastic cover. The glass dome, designed by the architect Sir Norman Foster, offers visitors unusual views over the capital until late at night. Since 1999, the German government has been using the Reichstag as its parliament, and it is one of the most prominent symbols of German reunification.

2 Ernst Reuter, Lord Mayor of West Berlin

1 Soviet War Memorial

4 US Military Police in front of the Brandenburg Gate

6 Russian Embassy

2 Soviet Graffiti in the Reichstag

4 "Mr. Gorbachev, open this gate!" Ronald Reagan and Helmuth Kohl in front of the Brandenburg Gate, 1987.

3
Wall Victims' Memorial
"White Crosses"

⌂ 1971 → Reichstagsufer, Map B 2
Ⓢ Unter den Linden In front of the east
entrance of the ▷ Reichstag, a small
stripe marks the ground where the former
Wall ran. White crosses by this marking
recall all those who lost their life while
attempting to escape to West Berlin since
1971. Guenter Litfin was the first victim
in August 1961, the last was Chris Gueffroy
in February 1989. In the future, the city
plans to erect a memorial for the victims
of the Wall close to these White Crosses.

4
Brandenburg Gate

⌂ Carl Gotthard Langhans, 1791
→ Pariser Platz, Map B2 Ⓢ Unter den
Linden The Brandenburg Gate was constructed in 1791 as a passage through
Berlin's city wall. Johann Gottfried
Schadow created the sculpture of the
goddess of peace Eirene to crown it.
After Bluecher's victory over Napoleon in
1814, she was reinterpreted as goddess
of victory. After the Second World War,
the Brandenburg Gate stood in the middle
of a wasteland. From then on, the Soviet
flag flew above Victoria. Protesters tore
down the flag on 17 June 1953, and
replaced it with the Tricolore in black,
red, and gold. From 1961 on, the gate
was marooned in the death strip of the
Berlin Wall, unapproachable for 28 years.
Ronald Reagan spoke the following words
on its west side on 12 June 1987:
**"General Secretary, Mr. Gorbatschow,
if you reach for freedom, if you desire
wealth for the Soviet Union and for
Eastern Europe, if you want to liberalize:
Come to this gate! Mr. Gorbatschow,
open this gate! Mr. Gorbatschow, tear
down this wall!"**
His demand seemed absurd, but Reagan
was to prove right. After the opening of
the Wall on 9 November 1989, hundreds
of people climbed onto it in front of the
Brandenburg Gate und brought about its
demise with hammers and chisels. Since
22 December 1989, the Brandenburg
Gate has been open to the public again.
It is the central symbol of German unity.

Ernst Reuter 1889–1953

Ernst Reuter was born in North Schles-
wig on 29 July 1889. He was severely
wounded during the First World War
and held in a Russian camp. There he
became acquainted with Lenin and
joined the Bolshevists, for whom he
worked as a people's commissioner
(Volkskommissar). Under his nom de
guerre of "Friesland", he was one of
the leading politicians of the Communist Party during the Weimar Republic.
Under the Social Democrats, he
became a leading figure in the public
transportation department and one
of the co-founders of Berlin's public
transportation system. The Nazis
imprisoned Reuter in the Lichtenburg
concentration camp in 1933, but he
managed to escape to Turkey and to
work in Ankara as professor of civil
engineering. In 1947, all members of
parliament of the City of Berlin elected him as Lord Mayor. The Soviet
authorities, however, refused to recognize him. Consequently, he could only
become mayor of West Berlin after
the division of the city in 1948.
During the Berlin blockade, he became
a symbol of the people of Berlin's will
to persist. In front of the ▷ Reichstag,
he appealed to the world community:
**"You, people of the world, you people
of the Americas, of England, of France,
look upon this city. Recognize that you
must not give up on this city and on
its people, for those who give up on
the people of Berlin, give up on a world,
and more, give up on themselves."**
Ernst Reuter died on 29 September
1953. His son Edzard Reuter later
became CEO of Daimler Benz AG.

TIME LINE OF BERLIN HISTORY 1945–2000

1939 At the beginning of the war, Berlin has 4.3 mill. inhabitants

1943 First severe air raids on Berlin

8 May 1945 End of Second World War

17 July 1945 Start of the Potsdam Conference

1948 Berlin Blockade

23 May 1949 Foundation of the Federal Republic of Germany (FRG)

7 October 1949 Foundation of the German Democratic Republic (GDR)

1953 People's Uprising 17 June

13 August 1961 Erection of Berlin Wall

1963 Kennedy visit

1967 Student Unrest, Ohnesorg is shot

1969 Construction of TV Tower

"Third Reich"   Federal Republic of Germany/

1945   1949   1961

5
Academy of the Arts of the GDR/Academy of the Arts

⌂ Benisch & Partner, 2003 → Pariser Platz 4, Map B3 Ⓢ Unter den Linden
The Academy of the Arts was founded in 1696, and has been located on Pariser Platz since 1907. Max Lieberman, its honorary president, stepped down in 1933, when the National Socialists forbid Jewish artists from pursuing their work. The building was assigned to Hitler's personal architect Albert Speer and his fellow commanders in 1937. After war damage, the GDR tore the front of the building down in the 1950s. The back served as a studio. The GDR founded its own Academy of the Arts in the Eastern sector of Berlin in 1950, situated at Robert-Koch-Platz 7.
Heinrich Mann was its first president, the dramatist Heiner Mueller its last as the GDR ended. Many artists banned under the NS government returned from exile and became members of the Academy, among them Bertolt Brecht and John Heartfield.
Likewise, an Academy of the Arts was founded in Berlin's West sector in 1954, and headed by the architect Hans Scharoun. The academy had its own home in the reconstructed Hansa district of town at Tiergarten from 1960 on. Both academies reunited in 1993. Since 2004, the reunited academy has had its new home on Pariser Platz. The building on Hanseatenstrasse is used for exhibitions.

6
Embassy of the Soviet Union/Russian Embassy

⌂ Anatoli Strichewski, 1952 → Unter den Linden 63–65, Map C3 Ⓢ Unter den Linden The first permanent diplomatic representation of Russia in Berlin was established in 1706, during the reign of Peter the Great. During the Second World War, the Nazis occupied the embassy building. The "Ministry of the East" was located there until bombs destroyed it. In 1949, the Soviet Union was the first occupation force to start the construction of a new building for the representation of its country, erecting an architectural monument to itself. The imposing building with two side wings is three times the size of the pre-war embassy. Long hallways and function rooms are decorated with glass mosaics, exquisite fabrics, woodwork and mirrors. The building now houses the Russian embassy.

7
Stasi – The Exhibition

→ Mauerstr. 38, Map C3 Ⓤ Mohrenstraße ◷ Mon–Sat 10–18
The ▷ **Ministry of State Security** (MfS – Ministerium fuer Staatssicherheit) was as the "sword and shield of the party",

Diverse markings of the former course of the Wall

1979 First occupations of houses, Kreuzberg	**1987** 750th year celebrations East and West Berlin	**3 October 1990** GDR joins FRG	
	Reagan visit		**1999** Government moves to Berlin
BERLINER MAUER 1961 – 1989			
		9 November 1989 Fall of Berlin Wall	
1971 Honecker succeeds Ulbricht	**1985** Exchange of agents, Glienecker Bruecke	**1987** Human rights activists protest, Zions Church	**1994** Occupation troops leave Berlin

German Democratic Republic   **Federal Republic of Germany**

1989

the SED dictatorship's foremost instrument of repression. The documentation "Stasi – the Exhibition" demonstrates the machinery of 40 years of continuous surveillance, manipulation, and persecution by the GDR regime. It includes, for example, glass jars, in which Stasi preserved particular odors of individual citizens of the GDR on fabric, to identify suspects with trained dogs.

8
National Front of the GDR/ Federal Ministry of Health and Social Security

⌂ Karl Reichle, 1936 → Wilhelmstr. 49/ Mauerstr. 45–53, Map C3 Ⓤ Mohrenstraße The suite of buildings was extended in 1936 under Joseph Goebbels to serve the "Ministry of Public Enlightenment and Propaganda". While Hitler's Chancellery was removed after the war, only the eagles and swastika symbols of the Nazis were removed from this building. Since the establishment of the GDR government on 7 October 1949, its first president Wilhelm Pieck held his office here, as did the National Council of the National Front. The National Front was an assembly of all political parties and mass organizations of the GDR under the leadership of the SED. Today, these buildings house the Federal Ministry of Health and Social Security.

9
Observation Tower and Remnants of the Wall Leipziger Platz

⌂ 1961 → Leipziger Platz, Stresemannstr., Map B4 Ⓢ Ⓤ Potsdamer Platz During the partition of Berlin, Potsdamer Platz and Leipziger Platz were located in the middle of the zone restricted by GDR boundaries. Antitank obstacles, barbed wire, and the Wall lined this once lively center of Berlin, rather than commerce displays and populated areas. World War II ruins, like the magnificent Wertheimer store, were systematically torn down on the GDR side, and underground stations were blocked off. Only a few remnants of the Wall have been preserved. Somewhat hidden behind new buildings stands one of Berlin's last observation towers in Erna-Berger-Strasse.

9 Surveillance tower on Leipziger Platz

Virchow ■

Reinhardtstr.

Parliament of Trees

34

Luisenstr.

3

Memorial to Victims of the Wall

Reichstag

2

Dorotheenstr.

Brandenburg Gate

4

Pariser Platz

Ⓢ

5

Behrenstr.

Memorial for the Murdered Jews of Europe

Course of the Wall

Ebertstr.

Death strip

Goethe ■

Rear Wall

Voßstr.

Leipziger Str.

Ⓢ Ⓤ Leipziger Platz

Bundesrat

Potsdamer Platz

9

Surveille border tower

11

Niederkirchnerstr.

10

Den unbekannten Opfern an der Mauer

Martin Gropius Building

3 Memorial Cross

Anhalter Station

Ⓢ

10
Remnants of the Wall at Niederkirchnerstrasse
⌂ 1961 → Niederkirchnerstr., Map B5
Ⓢ Ⓤ Potsdamer Platz At Nieder-kirchnerstrasse, a little dilapidated by "Wall hunters", stands one of the preserved pieces of the Berlin Wall. On the grounds behind were once the Reich Central Security Office (RSHA – Reichs-sicherheitshauptamt), the terror headquarters of the Third Reich. The exhibition "Topography of Terror" on this site informs visitors about one of the cruelest chapters of German history. A metal line on the ground indicates where the former Wall ran through the city of Berlin. The street in front of the Martin Gropius Building displays various suggestions by artists for marking the former Wall.

11
"House of Ministries"/ Federal Ministry of Finance
⌂ Ernst Sagebiel, 1936 → Wilhelmstr. 97, Map C3 Ⓤ Mohrenstraße The building conceived by the Architect Ernst Sagebiel served as Ministry of Aviation of the German Reich until 1945. This former government seat of Herman Goering survived the bombings almost untouched, which was the reason for its rapid takeover by new users. On 7 October 1949, the German Democratic Republic was founded here, and a few days later, Wilhelm Pieck was elected at this site as its first president. The building housed various ministries until 1989. The North wall was decorated with a tiled mural in 1952, representing the joy of workers over the reconstruction of the GDR. On 17 June 1953, protesting construction workers from ▷ Stalinallee marched to the "House of Ministries". A stone block at the corner of Wilhelm-/ Leipziger Strasse recalls this memorable day. After the demise of the GDR, the transitional privatization agency had its seat here, and was charged with transforming former GDR production facilities into private property. Since 1999, this house has been the main seat of the Federal Ministry of Finances. Guided tours around the building are available to groups.

10 A metal band marks the former course of the Wall in front of the Martin Gropius Building

7 Stasi exhibition

7 Glass jar with odor sample in the Stasi exhibition

10 Hole in the Wall on Niederkirchnerstrasse

11 Mural on tiles from the Meissner Porcelain Manufacture at the former "House of Ministries"

The Peoples' Uprising

The uprising of the people of 17 June 1953 is one of the most memorable days in German history. It was the first mass movement in the Soviet control, zone in which nearly one million citizens of the GDR participated.

The reasons for the dissatisfaction among the population of the GDR and the continuous escape of hundreds of thousands to the West were poor living standards and the undemocratic conditions of the country. On 23 May 1953, the SED leadership attempted to counteract the severe economic crisis, among other measures, with a 10% increase of working norms. Consequent protest actions occasioned the Soviet leaders to soften their measures and to demand "new directions", which were decided on 10 June by the SED Polit Office and ratified the following day by the Council of Ministries of the GDR. With this decision, social alleviation and more protection through justice was promised, but the increased work norms remained in place. The situation escalated on 15 June 1953. East Berlin workers from the construction site at the Friedrichshain Hospital went on strike. Fellow workers from the neighboring major construction site on ▷ **Stalinallee** joined them. The next day, it was no more question of just revocation of the increased work norm. By then, 10,000 demonstrators asked the government to step down, to release political prisoners, and to provide free elections. The workers called for a countrywide strike on 17 June.

"After the uprising of 17 June, the secretary of the Writers' Association had flyers distributed at Stalinallee. They read that the people had gambled with government confidence, lost it, and could regain it only by doubling their work efforts. Would it not be easier, under such conditions, for the government to ask the people to step down and to vote for another citizenry?"
(Bertolt Brecht, "Die Loesung")

17 JUNE 1953 IN BERLIN

- **Early Hours:** Soviet military units concentrate at the edge of East Berlin. SED leadership flees to Soviet Headquarters.
- **07:00** a.m.: Protest marches form. Strikes throughout the GDR.
- **09:00** a.m.: 25,000 demonstrators in front of the ▷ **"House of Ministries"**.
- **09:40** a.m.: 60,000 protestors on Potsdamer Platz.
- **10:00** a.m.: Soviet tanks advance toward the city center.
- **11:00** a.m.: Demonstrators rip the red flag from the Brandenburg Gate and burn it.
- **01:00** p.m.: A state of emergency is declared for East Berlin. Martial law is declared in areas of GDR. Soviet units intervene.
- **02:15** p.m.: First demonstrators shot on Alexanderplatz.
- **04:00** p.m.: US President Eisenhower discusses alternative reactions.
- **Into the evening:** Hundreds of demonstrators arrested.
- **09:00** p.m.: Ulbricht calls the uprising a "fascist attempt to provoke insurgence"
- **10:35** p.m.: West Berlin commemorates the dead and the wounded.

Countrywide, the peoples' uprising involved nearly 700 cities and communities and 600 factories and businesses. The people stormed numerous police stations, SED administrative sites, municipal buildings, and Stasi establishments. There were attempts to liberate inmates of 12 prisons. A total of at least 50 demonstrators died, 20 were summarily executed. During the weeks afterwards, thousands of arrests and condemnations to years of incarceration followed. The people should see the demonstration of might, which shunned no means to break the opposition. The FRG commemorated the event as the **"Day of German Unity"** from 1954 on.

Title page of "Stern" magazine in June 1953

Demonstrators at Potsdamer Platz defend themselves against overpowering Soviet tanks with stones

12 Soviet and US armored tanks at Checkpoint Charlie, 1961

13 Flags of the victorious powers

12 Steel helmets, GDR flags and gas masks: souvenir stall at Checkpoint Charlie

12 Checkpoint Charlie, 1961

12 Checkpoint Charlie with actors, 2005

Checkpoint Charlie

12
Checkpoint Charlie
⌂ 1961–1989 → Friedrich-/Zimmerstr.,
Map C4 Ⓤ Kochstraße After Berlin
was divided, Checkpoint Charlie became
the third site for Allied military, foreig-
ners, and workers at West Germany's
▷ **"Permanent Representation"** (StaeV –
Staendige Vertretung) to cross the border, following the two other sites Helmstedt (Alpha) and Dreilinden (Bravo).
Patrolling through all sectors by all four
occupation powers should have been
possible at all times. In October 1961,
however, the Soviet Allied forces suddenly denied US troops' entry into the
Soviet sector. American and Soviet tanks
faced each other in a showdown of
forces for several days at Checkpoint
Charlie, until the Soviet army ended the
provocation. The ▷ **Allied Museum** exhibits a Western Allies' observation station
of that time. The city plans to build a
museum dedicated to the Cold War.

13
Wall Museum "House at Checkpoint Charlie"
⌂ 1963 → Friedrichstr. 43–45, Map C4
Ⓤ Kochstraße ⊕ Mon–Sun 9–22
Originally, Rainer Hildebrandt (1914–
2004) founded the museum at Bernauer
Strasse in 1962, out of protest against
the erection of the Wall. High visitor
numbers occasioned its opening at Checkpoint Charlie in 1963. Even these many
years after reunification, this extensive
exhibition about the history of the Wall
in a private museum remains a tourist
attraction in Berlin.

14
Axel Springer Publishing House
⌂ Franz Heinrich Sobotka, Gustav
Mueller, Melchiorre Bega, Gino Franzi,
1966 → Kochstr. 50, Map D4 Ⓤ Kochstraße Axel Springer had his press building constructed in the former media
quarters of the city, right by the Wall,
in 1966, standing 68 meters high with
a golden brass facade. He refused to

recognize the division of the city as
something final. He committed his
editorial associates to abide by the four
axioms he published in 1967:
- Standing up for reunification
- Reconciliation with the Jewish people
- Refusal of political totalitarianism
- Defense of the social market economy.

All Springer publications had to write the
name "GDR" in quotation marks in order
to demonstrate the non-acceptance of
the East German state. The roof of the
media building had a neon display visible
to East Berliners with daily news from
the free press. The GDR government
answered in 1972 with the construction
of four 25-storey apartment buildings
near Leipziger Strasse. They intended
to block the view of the Springer news.
Since the 1960s, the 18th floor of the
press building has hosted the elite
"Springer-Club". Fresh pale-red roses
stand without fail under a photograph
of Axel Springer, who died in 1985.

15
Peter Fechter Memorial
⌂ 1999 → Zimmerstr. 26/27, Map D4
Ⓤ Kochstraße On 17 August 1962,
one year after the erection of the Wall,
the 18-year-old construction worker Peter
Fechter and a friend attempted their
escape to the West, near Zimmerstrasse.
Both had been able to force their bodies
through the barbed wire, when suddenly
border guards fired on them. The friend
managed to climb the man-size Wall
under fire and to pass to the other side.
Fechter's abdomen and back were hit. He
fell back to the East side and lay there
heavily wounded. West Berlin police were

only able to throw first-aid packages to the man calling for help. No GDR border guards or US soldiers from the nearby ▷ **Checkpoint Charlie** came to his aid. Fechter died about one hour later after heavy blood loss. Only then did border guards remove the body from the death strip, accompanied by shouts of **"Murderers, Murderers"** from West Berliners. A steel column now commemorates Peter Fechter at Zimmer-strasse.

16
International Media Center of the GDR/Federal Ministry of Justice
⌂ 1901, 1977 → Mohrenstr. 36/38, Map D3 Ⓤ Hausvogteiplatz The former "House Stern" housed the International Press Center of the GDR from 1977. It was here, during a press conference on November 9, 1989, that Guenter Schabowski, a member of the Politbureau, announced freedom to travel for GDR citizens. Too early. Originally, the news was intended for release the next day. Now this sudden news about the opening

of the Wall not only went around the world, but also into the living rooms of the people of East Berlin and of the GDR via the radio waves. Thousands of citizens of the GDR streamed to the border and were able to travel to the West for the first time a few hours later.

17
Central Committee of the SED/Foreign Office
⌂ Heinrich Wolff, 1939, Hans Kollhoff, Thomas Mueller, Ivan Reimann, 1999 → Werderscher Markt 1, Map D3 Ⓤ Hausvogteiplatz The rear part of the building complex at Werderscher Markt 1 was constructed in 1939 to extend the Reichsbank. Its safes contained the rich reserves captured by the "Third Reich" in the form of gold and valuable documents. From 1959, this building housed the Central Committee of the SED (ZK – Zentralkomitee), the center of power of the GDR. The ZK had the former teller halls transformed into a conference center. The second floor offered generous office suites for SED officials, with their own conference room and movie theater. In reality, and for forty years, only three men incorporated the central figures of power, namely as General Secretary of the ZK: Walter Ulbricht (1950–1971), Erich Honecker (1971–1989), and briefly Egon Krenz (1989). In this ZK building, the GDR Chamber of the People sessioned on 20 September 1990. A two-thirds majority voted for the reunification negotiations with the FRG and thus marked the end of the GDR. The old building was renovated in 1999 and extended at Werderstrasse. The whole complex now serves as the headquarters of the Foreign Office.

9 The Free German Press Inscription on the poster: Neues Deutschland "Nobody intends to build a wall!"

17 Foyer at the Foreign Office

17 ZK Entry

18 Palace of the Republic

The Berlin City Castle

18

**Palace of the Republic/
Berlin City Castle, Humboldt
Forum**

⌂ Ehrhardt Gisske, Heinz Graffunder,
Karl Ernst Swora, 1976/Reconstruction
2015 → Schlossplatz, Map E2

Ⓢ Ⓤ Alexanderplatz For half a century,
Prussian Kings and German Emperors
resided in the most important baroque
castle north of the Alps. The castle
caught fire during the Second World War,
but it survived the Allied bombing raids
relatively unscathed. For the new power
structure of the GDR, the edifice, which
had evolved since 1443, symbolized the
hated Prussian militarism. Just before
Ulbricht's detonation commandos approa-
ched on 7 September 1950, ready to
annihilate the castle, a final international
outcry formed in an attempt
to oppose the destruction.
There are other examples
in history about new reigns

in power and about their way of moving
into the edifices of the former reign.
Neither Lenin nor Stalin considered it
necessary to detonate the Kremlin as
Symbol of the tsarist monarchy. A huge
parade ground replaced the castle.
Designs to build a tall building for the
government or a "Tower of Signals"
were discarded. In 1972, Erich Honecker
decided the construction of the Palace
of the Republic, a hall in glass and gold
serving several purposes. Thousands of
round lamps lined the foyer, soon earning
the building the nickname **"Erich's lamp
store"** (Erichs Lampenladen). The small
hall hosted the Chamber of the People,
the powerless parliament of the GDR. The
large conference hall with 5,000 seats
and many functions offered space for any
conceivable function. Generally, the house
was conceived as a "House of the
People" (Volkshaus) serving multi-
fold events with its countless
thematic spaces and clubs,

18 West facade of the City Castle with Berlin Cathedral in the background, 1933

> "The detonation of the city castle was insanity. If Berlin were a history book, it would be missing many pages. One does not rip pages out of history books, even when the pages displease."
> (Renzo Piano, Architekt, 2000)

a theater, a bowling hall and art exhibitions. After reunification, the palace remained just a steel skeleton, which had survived asbestos sanitation. The round outlines are the only reminders of the former symbol of the GDR on the front and of the building's uses. After demolition of the palace, plans foresee a rebirth of the castle in modern form by 2015. Plans feature a "Humboldt Forum" which should join the Museum Island to form a site for art, culture, and communication. The visitor center at Hausvogteiplatz 3–4 displays information about the project by the "Berlin Castle" development association.

Walter Ulbricht 1893–1973

Walter Ulbricht, born in Leipzig and having experienced the First World War, joined the German Communist Party (KPD) in 1918. While the National Socialists (NS) were in power, he continued his work for the exiled party in Paris, Prague, and Moscow. In May 1945, he returned to the destroyed Berlin, heading the "Ulbricht Group". He was committed to reforming society after the Soviet model, part of which was the inception of a Socialist United Party (SED – Sozialistische Einheitspartei Deutschlands). **"It should have a democratic appearance, but we have to hold everything in our hands,"** was Ulbricht's message to his comrades. He had a decisive influence on the foundation of the German Democratic Republic in 1949 in that he had all essential government positions of power controlled by the SED. As First Secretary of the SED Central Committee and as head of government, he forced the socialist remodeling of cities. Significant cultural monuments fell victim to his relentlessly blind ideological commitment to demolition, among those the ▷ **City Castle of Berlin**, the ▷ **Schinkel Academy of Construction**, the Leipzig University Church of 1240, and the Potsdam Garnison Church. Despite Ulbricht's declaration on 15 June 1961 that nobody had the intention to build a Wall, the demarcation of the Soviet occupation zone began under his leadership on 13 August 1961, and with that the construction of the Berlin Wall. "Health reasons" occasioned his replacement as SED Party Chairman by Erich Honecker in 1971. Ulbricht died on 1 August 1973 in Doellnsee near Berlin.

Detonation of the City Castle, 1950

18 Foundations of the City Castle in front of the Palace

19 Portal of the former State Council Building

18 Erich Honecker and Egon Krenz (front left) at the X. Parliament of the FDJ in the Palace of the Republic, 1976

19
State Council Building of the GDR/ European School of Management and Technology

⌂ Roland Korn, Hans Erich Bogatzky, 1964 → Schlossplatz 1, Map E3
Ⓤ Hausvogteiplatz The State Council Building was one of the most prominent addresses of East Berlin. Between 1964 and 1989, it housed the office of the heads of the government council, Walter Ulbricht, Willi Stoph, Erich Honecker, and Egon Krenz. The modern building looks unusual with the fourth portal of the City Castle protruding from its center. The dates "1713/1963" at its top suggest an original. In reality, the portal is a copy. For the SED, this spot was important, because Karl Liebknecht declared the **"German Socialist Republic"** (Sozialistische Republik Deutschland) from here on 9 November 1918. The interior design is largely preserved in its original conception. The staircase displays a huge glass painting with depictions of the workers' movement. Between 1989 and 2001, Gerhard Schroeder used this building as his interim chancellery. Nowadays, a private college prepares managers in the tough everyday realities of capitalism in this building.

20
Ministry of Foreign Affairs of the GDR/Schinkel Academy of Construction

⌂ Josef Kaiser, Herbert Aust, 1966, Karl Friedrich Schinkel, 1836 → Schinkelplatz, Map D3 Ⓤ Hausvogteiplatz Karl Friedrich Schinkel created the Construction Academy (Bauakademie), the first significant functional architecture in Germany, in 1836. The 1950s saw the reconstruction of the academy, which had been damaged during the Second World War. In 1961/62 the academy had to make way for an 11-storey building for the Ministry of Foreign Affairs of the GDR. After reunification, the Foreign Ministry building was demolished again. The "Development Association of the Academy of Construction" (Foerderverein Bauakademie) supported reconstruction of a corner front of the academy. Total reconstruction is part of future plans.

The SED

The Socialist Unity Party of Germany (SED – Sozialistische Einheitspartei Deutschlands) formed in the ▷ **Admiralspalast** at Friedrichstrasse 101 in April 1946, as a result of a forced merger of the KPD with the East German SPD. The Social Democrat Otto Grotewohl and the Communist Wilhelm Pieck symbolically shook hands. The SED symbol depicts this act. The Central Committee was the top organ of the party, headed by the Polit Bureau and the General Secretary. The National Front was under the command of the SED, and assembled the parties and mass organizations of the GDR. The SED adopted the new name of "Party of Democratic Socialism" (PDS – Partei des Demokratischen Sozialismus) in 1989. Since 2005, its name has been "The Left Party. PDS" (Die Linkspartei. PDS). Its headquarters are in the ▷ **Karl Liebknecht House**.

Socialist Unity Party of Germany

"The Party" (Louis Fuernberg)
The Party, it is always right.
And, comrades, thus be it forever.
For who fights for right,
Is always right.
Against lies and exhortation.
He who insults life
Is stupid or bad.
He who defends humankind
Is always right.
Thus, out of Lenin's spirit
Grows, joined by Stalin,
The Party, the Party, the Party!

21 Changing the guard from the regiment "Friedrich Engels" in front of the Neue Wache, 1969

24 World Time Clock in front of the TV Tower

20 Replica of the Construction Academy, 2005

21 Snow on the sculpture "Mother with Dead Son"

25 Illuminated GDR advertising on Alexanderplatz

21
New Watchhouse
⌂ Karl Friedrich Schinkel, 1818 → Unter den Linden 4, Map D2 Ⓤ Hausvogtei-platz The New Watchhouse (Neue Wache), designed by Schinkel, served as a royal watchhouse and a memorial for the Wars of Liberation until 1918. The 1958 inauguration reassigned it as a **"Memorial for the Victims of Fascism and Militarism".** An eternal flame burned in a crystal cube in the memorial chamber. A double post of the NVA guard squadron "Friedrich Engels" guarded the entrance, presenting their machine guns. Since 1993, the New Watchhouse has been Germany's central memorial site for the victims of war and tyranny. The former Chancellor Helmut Kohl chose Kaethe Kollwitz's rendering of the "Pieta" for the interior hall.

22
House of Democracy/House of the German Association of Administrators
→ Friedrichstr. 165–170, Map C3 Ⓤ Französische Straße After the SED stepped down, the political leaders felt pressure from protest movements to enter negotiations with opposition groups. This event occasioned the first meeting of the "Central Round Table" in Berlin on 7 December 1989. The defenders of citizens' rights demanded the democrati-zing of the GDR, the disbanding of the Stasi, and of the control over government decrees. The political transformations activated a true revolution. The power structures of the SED were not only reformed but actually destroyed. On 10 January 1990, the political opposition groups were given the building of the SED Central Command of Berlin-Mitte at Friedrichstrasse 165 for their purposes. The "House of Democracy" served as a coordination and working site for the "New Forum", the "Green League", "Democracy Now", and many more groups. At the first free GDR elections on 18 March 1990, however, the movements for citizens' rights had no chance against the big parties supported by the West. In 1999, the citizens' rights groups left their quarters to the German Association of Administrators, who financed a new building. A new, larger "House of Demo-cracy and Human Rights" was built in Greifswalder Strasse.

23
Marx-Engels-Forum
⌂ Ludwig Engelhardt, 1986 → Karl-Liebknecht-Str./Spandauer Str., Map E2 Ⓢ Ⓤ Alexanderplatz After the Second World War, a field of ruins stretched from the City Castle to Alexanderplatz, lined with charred apartment blocks. The last symbol of the old city outlines still stands with the 13th-century St. Mary's Church (Marienkirche). Opposite it, the Marx-Engels-Forum was inaugurated in 1986. In its center stands the Ludwig Engelhardt sculpture of the founders of "scientific socialism", Karl Marx and Friedrich Engels. Originally, the SED Party had planned a 36-m-high sculpture. Engelhardt finally received a commission for the more modest version. He created the two-figure sculpture during nearly ten years of work on the island of Usedom, which is now a listed monument.

25 Mural at the "House of the Teacher"

"Berlin Alexanderplatz"

24
Television Tower
Hermann Henselmann, Fritz Dieter, Guenter Franke, 1969 → Panoramastr. 1, Map E2 Ⓢ Ⓤ Alexanderplatz

In 1959, Hermann Henselmann conceived the "Tower of the Signals" for the new center of Berlin, for the architecture competition under the name of "Socialist Transformation of the Capital of the GDR". Ten years later, this tower turned into the Television Tower, as a new symbol of East Berlin. At 368 meters, it is the second-highest structure in Europe. The 7-storey sphere features a rotating tele-café.

This former socialist object of prestige, of all structures, reflects a Christian symbol easily visible from far around: The sun forms a sparkling cross of light in the metal facets of the sphere. The entrance hall exhibits representations of the highest towers of the world in typical GDR design.

The highest structure overall is the 628.8-m antenna of the KVLY TV station in North Dakota in the United States.

25
"House of the Teacher" and Congress Hall/Berlin Congress Center
Hermann Henselmann, 1964 → Alexanderplatz 4, Map F2 Ⓢ Ⓤ Alexanderplatz

Alexanderplatz and its surrounding buildings were largely destroyed during the Second World War. Only the Berolinahaus and the Alexanderhaus designed by Peter Behrens were restored. All around, unattractive Plattenbauten (prefabricated concrete blocks) arose during the 1960s. A notable exception was the Hermann Henselmann design for the "House of the Teacher" and its neighboring congress hall. Until 1990, the building served as a center of culture, teaching, and information. Walter Womacka's wall art, 127 meters long and made of 800,000 glass stones, depicts the model daily life of socialist youth. This glass ensemble is now regarded as one of the classics of modern GDR art and is a listed building. Many buildings around Alexanderplatz are on the demolition list. Soon, skyscrapers should mark the skyline of the city at this spot.

26 A former department store served the SED as party headquarters after the war

26
Party Center and Party Archive of the SED "House of Unity"
⌂ Bauer und Friedlaender, 1929
→ Torstr. 1, Map F1 Ⓤ Rosa-Luxemburg-Platz In 1929, the Jewish business-person Hermann Golluber had a department store constructed at the current Torstrasse 1. The Nazi government ordered the sale of the building in 1942. Under SED rule, the former department store served as seat of the Central Committee (ZK) for several years, under the name of "House of Unity". Memorial plaques at its entrance remind passers-by of the times of Wilhelm Pieck and Otto Grotewohl holding joint power as heads of the SED. The political administrators convicted political dissenters to death here and organized the vindication campaign against the insurgents of 17 June 1953. Between 1959 and 1995, the Institute for Marxism-Leninism and the Party Archive of the SED used this building. Plans for the future include a museum of the "anatomy of the SED dictatorship".

27
Karl Liebknecht House
⌂ Keibel, 1912 → Kleine Alexanderstr. 28, Map F1 Ⓤ Rosa-Luxemburg-Platz In 1926, the Communist Party (KPD) acquired the preserved office building on Kleine Alexanderstrasse 28 and named it after its founder Karl Liebknecht. Among others, the Central Committee and the newspaper "Red Flag" (Rote Fahne) had their offices here. During the Nazi era, the SA used the building as "Horst Wessel House". After the war, leaders of the Communist Party returned from Soviet exile to Berlin and later gathered in the SED. Following its renaming in 1989/90, the SED was called "Party of Democratic Socialism" (PDS), and since 2005, it has gone under the name of "The Left Party. PDS" (Die Linkspartei. PDS).

The "Work of the Workers"

370 m
360 m
350 m
310 m
300 m
290 m
280 m
270 m
260 m
250 m
240 m
230 m
220 m
210 m
200 m
190 m
180 m
170 m
160 m
150 m
140 m
130 m
120 m
110 m
100 m
90 m
80 m
70 m
60 m
50 m
40 m
30 m
24 Depiction of the TV Tower in its entry hall — 20 m
10 m

25 Mural at the "House of Tourism" on Alexanderplatz

29 PermRepr of the Rhineland in Berlin

27 Listed building: Karl Liebknecht House

29 Scharoun's studio

29 Garden pavilion of the Permanent Representation

29 Former office of the head of the PermRepr

The "Permanent Representation"

28
New Synagogue/
Centrum Judaicum

⌂ Knoblauch, Stueler, 1866 → Oranienburger Str. 28-30, Map D1 Ⓢ Oranienburger Straße ⊕ Sun-Thu 10-18,
Fri 10-14 During the pogroms of November 1938, the New Synagogue was set on
fire and desecrated. It suffered additional
heavy damage during the bombing of
Berlin. In 1958, the GDR demolished the
main tower with the magnificent golden
dome, and the synagogue stood in ruins
from then on. The SED leadership was
not interested in rebuilding it. More than
that, it denounced the Jewish community
from time to time as an "agent of US
imperialism". Until its demise, the GDR
maintained no diplomatic relations with
Israel and paid no reparations. In the
hopes of brushing up his relations with
the USA, Erich Honecker decided in favor
of the reconstruction of the synagogue in
1988, financed by international donations.
Shortly before the Wall fell in 1989, the
Jewish community in the GDR counted
a mere 372 members.
Today, the New Synagogue houses the
Centrum Judaicum with the archives of
the history of the Jewish people of Berlin.

29
Permanent Representation
of the FRG in the GDR/
Federal Ministry of Education
and Research

⌂ 1913, Hans Scharoun, 1949, Jourdan &
Mueller, 2000 → Hannoversche Str. 28-30,
Map C1 Ⓤ Oranienburger Tor Although
the building may not appear so, it looks
back on a long history. Built in 1913 as
military complex for the Cavalry Artillery
Guard, it burned down completely in the
Second World War. The architect Hans
Scharoun had the ruin remodeled in 1947
for the Academy (Bauakademie). Under
his leadership, the Institute for Construction Engineering coordinated the reconstruction of East Berlin and the GDR from
here. The Scharoun studio under its roof
has been preserved to this day. During

the summer of 1974, the "Permanent
Representation of the Federal Republic
of Germany (FRG) in the German Democratic Republic (GDR)" (StaeV – official
abbreviation for "Staendige Vertretung")
moved into the building. The first head
of the mission was Guenter Gaus. Klaus
Boelling succeeded him, then Hans-Otto
Braeutigam and Franz Bertele. Their former office is still intact in its original
state, for visitors. In the back of the
building stands a soundproof garden
house in the style of the chancellery in
Bonn, which sheltered citizens of the
GDR seeking emigration from 1975 on.
This was a reason for the Stasi to survey
the "Permanent Representation" constant-
ly from neighboring buildings. Several
GDR police officers stood close to the
building, hoping for a chance to catch
potential refugees. Now, after extensions
and transformations of the building, the
Ministry of Education and of Research is
based in it. Since 1997, Berlin has had a
"Permanent Representation" again. It now
carries the suffix "Rheinland", stands
opposite Friedrichstrasse station on
Schiffbauerdamm 8, and one can order
"Koelsch" beer there. The pub already
existed in Bonn and was a meeting point
favored by journalists and politicians. The
owners initially opposed the government's
relocation to the new capital. Later they
followed their regular patrons. Among
numerous relics of German-German
history, one can meet some well-known
faces from politics in the StaeV.

"Sozialismus – schön und gut
Aber was man uns hier aufsetzt
Das ist de r falsche Hut!"

("Socialism – all fine and good, but what they put on our head is the wrong hat."),
From Wolf Biermann's manuscript "Don't await better times", 1974)

30
Emil Fischer Auditorium of the Humboldt University
→ Hessesche Str. 1–2, Map C1 Ⓤ Oranienburger Tor In 1963/64, Professor Robert Havemann held a colloquium series about "scientific aspects of philosophical problems" in the chemistry auditory of the East Berlin Humboldt University. In this series, he pleaded for a democratic socialism and for freedom of expression as an SED member. Consequently, he was dismissed from the university and expelled from the Party. In 1976, the Stasi actually arrested Havemann in his residence in Gruenheide. A memorial plaque in the Emil Fischer Auditorium commemorates this event.

31
Wolf Biermann's Residence
→ Chausseestr. 131, Map C1 Ⓤ Oranienburger Tor At the age of 16, Wolf Biermann moved from Hamburg to East Berlin in 1953. He started out composing songs at the Berlin Ensemble. He called himself a "songwriter" after his ideal the "play writer" Bertolt Brecht, who lived not far away. Many famous literary personalities and critics of the regime, including Robert Havemann, met in Biermann's home in the 1960/70s. His songs and texts were already prohibited at that time. During a tour of West Germany in 1976, the SED used the chance to get rid of this critical voice and recalled his citizenship, which made his return impos-

32 The "Prussian Icarus"-Wolf Biermann on Weidendammer Bridge

sible. Unexpected protests came from significant writers and artists of the GDR, but Biermann was only granted one more visit in 1982, to his ill friend Havemann.

32
Bertolt Brecht Residence / Brecht-Weigel Memorial Site and Cemetery Dorotheen- staedtischer Friedhof
→ Chausseestr. 125, Map C1 Ⓤ Oranien- burger Tor ⊙ Tue – Fri 10 – 12, Sun 11 – 18
In 1948, after many years in exile, the dramatist Bertolt Brecht returned to Berlin. He lived with his wife Helene Weigel at Chausseestrasse for three years – an apartment of "decent size", as he wrote to his editor Suhrkamp. Since 1978, the rooms have housed the Brecht-Weigel memorial site, with their library of nearly 4,000 books and a func- tion room.
Helene Weigel and Bertolt Brecht found their last resting place in the nearby Dorotheenstaedtischer Fried-hof close to many other famous personalities. Among them are the philosopher Georg W. F. Hegel, the architects Friedrich Schinkel and Johann Gottfried Schadow, and the writers Theodor Fontane, Heinrich Mann, and Heiner Mueller.

33
Border Checkpoint Invalidenstrasse
⌂ 1961 – 1989 → Sandkrugbrücke, Map B1 Ⓢ Berlin Hauptbahnhof
The border checkpoint Invalidenstrasse was the tragic setting for an escape attempt by twelve young women and men on 12 May 1963. In an omnibus, they wanted to break through to West Berlin at this controlled point. Pierced by machine gun fire by the GDR border patrol, the bus got stuck in a street blockade close to the Western sector. The wounded refugees were immediately arrested. Bricked-off doors on the south side of Invalidenstrasse are the last traces of the border crossing. A glass stand on Sandkrugbruecke now informs visitors about the escape attempt.

Bertolt Brecht 1898–1956
Bertolt Brecht was born in Augsburg on 10 February 1898. As early as 1918, he directed his first own theater play, **"Baal"**. From 1926 on, he lived in Berlin and worked as dramatist at Max Reinhardt's German Theater. His work as a freelance writer and thea- ter director during the year 1926 increasingly involved Brecht with Marxist writing, and he embraced communist thinking. His theater play **"The Threepenny Opera"** made his international breakthrough in 1928 (music by Kurt Weill).
Brecht had to leave Germany in 1933, after Hitler came to power. He lived mostly in Scandinavia and the USA. During his exile, he wrote some of his most famous works, among them **"The Life of Galilei"**. In November 1948, Brecht returned to East Berlin and founded the Berliner Ensemble the following year with his wife Helene Weigel. The stage for this ensemble was the German Theater, which witnessed the play **"Mother Courage and her Children"** in 1949. From 1954 on, the Berliner Ensemble staged its plays on Schiffbauerdamm (today Bertolt Brecht Platz 1). Fritz Cremer's sculpture of Brecht now stands at this place. From 1950, Brecht was a member of the ▷ **Academy of the Arts of the GDR**. Bertolt Brecht died of a heart attack on August 14, 1956. He and his wife Helene Weigel are buried in the ▷ **Cemetery Dorotheenstaedtischer Friedhof** in Berlin-Mitte.

37 Soviet MIG jets thunder over the Congress Hall in the Tiergarten, 7 April 1965

32 Entry to the Brecht House

37 House of the Cultures of the World

35 Palace of Tears

33 Bus pierced by bullets at Invalidenstrasse border crossing, 12 May 1963

34
"Parliament of Trees against War and Violence"

⌂ Ben Wargin, 1990 → Schiffbauerdamm, Map B 2 Ⓢ Ⓤ Friedrichstraße
Opposite the Reichstag, on the banks of
the river Spree stands the "Parliament of
Trees against War and Violence" conceived
by Ben Wargin. Different trees from the
16 German federal states grow on a green
plain. Painted Wall segments mark the
route where the former Wall ran and
juxtaposed large granite plaques bear the
names of those who died at the Wall.

35
Border Checkpoint Friedrichstrasse Station and "Palace of Tears"

⌂ Carl Theodor Bordfuehrer, 1925
→ Friedrichstr. 98 – 99, Map C 2
Ⓢ Ⓤ Friedrichstraße Due to the construction of the Wall, Friedrichstrasse
station became the border crossing for
underground and long-distance train tra-
velers from the West in 1961. For East
Berlin passengers, this was the final
station. A labyrinth of visual barricades,
hallways and windowless rooms led tra-
velers to the passport hall, the so-called
"Palace of Tears". "Border officials" with
cold faces checked passports before the
visitors had to exchange a minimum sum
of currency. In the opposite direction,
sad-looking East Germans said good-bye
to their visitors from the West. The
underground train S 2 was forbidden territory to East Berliners. The train from the
West stopped exclusively at Friedrichstrasse. The metro stations on East
Berlin territory became ghost stations,
and included Potsdamer Platz, Unter den
Linden, Oranienburger Strasse, and
Nordbahnhof. The trains passed slowly
along barely-lit platforms guarded by
GDR border patrols with machine guns.
During the 1990s, the station at Friedrichstrasse was refurbished with great
effect. At the spot where intershops once
sold duty-free goods to West Berliners
now stands a supermarket, open until
late at night – the greatest attraction.
The "Palace of Tears" hosts cultural
events till 2006.

36
Admiral Palace

⌂ Heinrich Schweitzer, Alexander Die-
penbrock, 1910 → Friedrichstr. 101 / 102,
Map C 2 Ⓢ Ⓤ Friedrichstraße At its
height during the golden 20s, the Admiral
Palace sported an ice arena, variety clubs,
a luxury swimming pool and a theater.
Its initial construction served as an extension of the Admiral Garden swimming
pool, which had access to its own brine
spring in the middle of Berlin. The building survived the Second World War
almost unscathed. At this spot, on 21 / 22
April 1946, the forced union between the
KPD and the East SPD took place. The
handshake between Wilhelm Pieck and
Otto Grotewohl was the beginning of the
SED. At the same spot, Friedrich Ebert
was elected first Lord Mayor of East Berlin in 1948. Until the Wall came down,
the Metropol-Theater, among other features, stood behind the richly ornamented
but crumbling front of the building.
Following old models, the House of Tra-
ditions (Traditionshaus) is being restored
thoroughly and re-inaugurated in 2006 as
temple of entertainment – just like in the
old days with a Grand Café and a brine
spring in the original Art Nouveau style.

37
Congress Hall / House of the Cultures of the World

⌂ Hugh A. Stubbins, 1957 → John-
Foster-Dulles-Allee 10, Map A 2
Ⓢ Ⓤ Berlin Hauptbahnhof The Congress Hall was founded in 1957 as gift
from the USA to West Berlin to mark the
International Construction Exhibition (In-
ternationale Bauausstellung). On 7 April
1965, far away from Bonn, the West
German government met here. It was a
demonstration that West Berlin was part
of the federal republic. Consequently,
500 Soviet fighter jets flew low in several
formations right over the Congress Hall.
The government representatives could not
understand their own words and decided
to end the session. In 1980, the roof of
the Congress Hall crumbled due to a cor-
roded steel structure. Since 1989, the
building has served as the "House of the
Cultures of the World" for various events.

Berlin's "rubble women" at work among Second World War ruins, Spring 1945

Rising from the Ruins

The Second World War, which was started in Berlin, had brought death and misery over the whole of Europe. After the capitulation of the German military on 8 May 1945, the former capital of the Reich was a ruin. Some walls still showed old graffiti of the type "The Fuehrer ordered, we obey," and next to it on another wall of a ruin fresh paint read, "Hitler took 12 years for this." 70 percent of the center was destroyed. More than 1.5 million people, almost half of the inhabitants left in Berlin, were homeless.

Men capable of work had died on the fronts, were wounded or were held in allied POW camps. That left women to fight for daily survival. They worked as "rubble women" to support their families, consisting almost exclusively now of the elderly and children. They were highly dependent on income and on higher rations of food. Berlin alone employed more than 60,000 rubble women, officially hired as "aids in the construction trade". They faced the challenge of removing more than 80 million cubic meters of rubble from the ruins, and they faced the constant danger of damaged remains of structures crumbling over them and unexploded munitions blowing up under their feet. They carried granite blocks and steel girders. The rubble traveled in buckets from hand to hand to removal transportation sites, while reusable bricks had to be cleaned of mortar with hammers. The unprecedented exemplary and tireless labor by these women became the symbol of reconstruction. A memorial honors them in the Hasenheide Park.

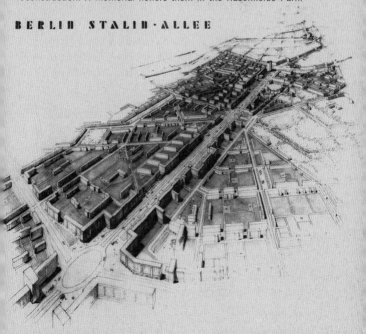

BERLIN STALIN-ALLEE

Award-winning model by Egon Hartmann of the Collective Henselmann for the "Stalinallee Competition", 1951

THE BERLIN EMERGENCY PROGRAM IS CARRIED OUT WITH THE HELP OF THE MARSHALL PLAN

ALBERT SPEER'S "CONSTRUCTION TEAM"

After the war, many destroyed German cities viewed a total break with the past as the only possible way forward. But in Hamburg, Hannover, Duesseldorf, or Nuremberg it was precisely Hitler's former architects and city planners who now conducted the reconstruction. These reconstruction men were recruited from Albert Speer's former "Reconstruction Team", which had been founded in 1944 in Wriezen near Berlin and which had begun planning preparatory reconstruction for after the "final victory". This personal network had subsisted into the postwar years, even though the war was lost, while Speer was incarcerated in the

▷ Spandau prison for war criminals. The plans from Nazi times for "traffic-compatible" inner cities and less formal construction going beyond historically grown city structures were now put into action.

"COLLECTIVE PLAN"

When Germany started over in 1945, the architect Hans Scharoun became Berlin's first post-war head of construction. During the 1920s, he was a member of the avant-garde "Neues Bauen" movement. He and his team presented the "Collective Plan" in 1946, with a design for a totally new city structure. This plan suggested that only a few historical buildings should be preserved, as well as the Unter den Linden boulevard. All other buildings were to be made available for creating space for four East-West-oriented "functional strips" for federal and public institutions. A lattice of highways was to overlay the system. Scharoun's vision proved generally impractical. His traffic conception, however, was realized in part, with raised highways cutting through the body of the city in broad strands.

THE "CULTURE OF DESTRUCTION"

No less than five governments marked the skyline of the city of Berlin during the 20th century, from imperial times, through the Weimar Republic and the "Third Reich", to the GDR, and finally the FRG. Each system in power attempted to

The exhibition "Berlin Plans – First Report" at the Berlin City Castle shows models by Scharoun and others, 1946

overcast or even eliminate the memorial sites of its forerunners with its own creations.

1945 and the destruction of the Second World War were followed by a policy of demolition during the 1950s. Partly decreed by the Allies, the city eliminated testaments to Nazi history. Hitler's New Reich Chancellery was torn down as along with the Prince Albert Palace, in which the Gestapo and SS central offices had resided. However, twelve synagogues, which had survived the Nazis and allied bombing raids only partly damaged, were taken down. Historical buildings in East and West alike fell victim to the craze of destruction, including the ▷ **Berlin City Castle**, ▷ **Schinkel Construction Academy** and Anhalter station. In some parts of the city, sanitation experts had whole districts pulled down, among them the medieval Nikolai district and the Fischerkiez, as well as the late-nineteenth-century housing in Wedding. Some of the grounds from which historical buildings were removed still stand vacant today.

"ALL AROUND THE ZOO"

Over 100 designs were submitted to the October 1947 competition "All around the Zoo". Not one of the architects planned the conservation of the ruins of the ▷ **Kaiser Wilhelm Memorial Church** which, after the erection of the Wall, turned into the symbol of West Berlin.

Hermann Henselmann 1905–1995
Stalinist neoclassicism, visible in the Karl-Marx-Allee (former Stalinallee), as well as the futuristic design of the television tower marked Hermann Henselmann's range of architectural styles, as spear-headers for GDR construction. Henselmann grew up in the Harz mountains as the son of a carpenter. He completed a carpenter's apprenticeship and left, rather than taking over his father's business, to study interior design and architecture in Berlin. In 1930 he built the Villa Kenwin in the vicinity of Geneva, a radically modern design, which could well have been designed by his great role model Le Corbusier. The Nazis ousted him from the Reich Chamber of Education in Arts as a "half-Jew" in 1941. After the war, he became Director of the University for Construction Art of Weimar, the foundation site of the Bauhaus School in 1919. In 1951 he participated in designs for Berlin's ▷ **Stalinallee**. His modern visions displeased the SED leadership and were dismissed, among them the high-rise building at Weberwiese. Consequently, Henselmann appeased himself with party line and advanced from to chief of construction of East Berlin from 1954–1959. The ▷ **Television Tower** on Alexanderplatz materialized, based on his conception "Tower of Signals" of ten years earlier. Here, his ▷ **"House of the Teacher"** was also built in 1964, reflecting international modern style. The probably most prominent architect of the GDR style of construction died in 1995 in the reunited city of Berlin.

Model for an airport at Zoo train station, 1948

The "Tower of Signals"

The reconstruction of other buildings on Breitscheidplatz was not planned either. The ideal of the times called for a "car-compatible city" with crossing-free traffic concentration points and with overhead bridges for pedestrians. Sergius Ruegenberg even planned an inner-city airport in the place of the zoological garden, with its own highway connection and a conference hall. The structure of the city, which had evolved over hundreds of years, was entirely ignored. None of the submitted conceptions, however, was to be built. In 1963–65, the Europa Center came into existence on Breidscheidplatz. The square was transformed into a spacious pedestrian area in 1982–84.

Instead of a high-rise building for the government requested by the SED for the castle space, Henselmann conceived a 300-m-high, futurist "Tower of Signals" with a UFO-like Congress Hall in front. This initially cost him his position as Chief Architect of East Berlin. In 1969, his slightly transformed, now 368-m-high TV Tower was built on Alexanderplatz.

WEALTH VS. IDEOLOGY

On 3 April 1948, the Marshall plan – named after US Foreign Minister George Marshall – poured billions of dollars into Europe to aid its reconstruction. Its aims were not only to revitalize the market with raw materials, goods, and investment funds, but to provide for enough material wealth to create a sense of well-being and quality of life to rid society of old Nazi ideologies as well as preventing the onslaught of Communism. This aid package laid the foundations for the ensuing "economic miracle" in the western part of Germany. The Soviet zone pursued the aim of building a communist society modeled on Stalinist ideals. The

"Tower of Signals"

Old Museum

Congress Hall

Red Town Hall

Marien Church

Town Hall Arcades

Design by the Henselmann Kollektiv for the "socialist reconstruction" of the East-Berlin Center, 1959

focus was initially dominated by demolition. Whole factories were rigorously
transported to the USSR, depriving the
East of material means for a successful
restart for a long time. The "National
Reconstruction Organization" started a
mass initiative for unpaid work partici-
pation in the reconstruction of Berlin
in 1952, supported by a reconstruction
lottery and volunteer reconstruction
savings. Up to 1967, GDR people con-
tributed 80 million voluntary hours of
work in reconstruction, amounting to
380 million GDR marks.

The Hansa District

The federal government initiated the
international construction exhibition
InterBau in the Hansa District of Tiergarten in 1957. It was the largest commitment to reconstruction in West Berlin.
Its initiators intended to demonstrate
their determination to the world and to
present a "city of tomorrow" in contrast
to the "fake veneer" of the Stalinallee.
53 architects from 13 countries participated, among them Walter Gropius,

Construction poster for the Weberwiese
tower block, 1951

Alvar Aalto, Wassili Luckhardt, Oscar
Niemeyer, and Hans Scharoun. They were
all involved in the concept of a loosely
structured inner city with high-rise apartment buildings and detached homes
embedded in green spaces. Among the
demonstration objects was Le Corbusier's
Unité d'habitation (apartment unit).

The little BIG BLOCK Construction Master Type 2: the "Platte" as a toy for GDR youngsters

THE "PLATTE"

Berlin's first pre-fabricated concrete apartment buildings date back to 1926 and are still standing undamaged in Splanemannstrasse in the Lichtenberg area. The construction process originated in the Netherlands. Only after Stalin's death did the GDR import this modern mass-construction style using industrially prefabricated plates, implementing it extensively. The different versions of the "Platte" carried names like "Typ P1" – Plattenbau 1 (Type P1 – plate construction 1), or later "WBS 70" – Wohnbauserie 70 (Construction Series 70), and sounded as unimaginative as they looked. Hermann Henselmann attempted to release the prefabricated constructions from their stern norm and managed to produce the swing-line design of the high-rise buildings at Leninplatz in 1970, now Platz der Vereinten Nationen. As part of the GDR apartment construc-

tion programs, whole districts of prefabricated buildings were built in the 1970s, such as in Marzahn and Hellersdorf. The 1980s witnessed attempts at decorating these constructions with mosaic, stucco, and corner balconies, to better integrate their appearance with their historical surroundings in the Nikolai district, or on Gendarmenmarkt in Mitte. In 1985, Hitler's Reich Chancellery and "Fuehrerbunker" on the almost completely war-destroyed Wilhelmstrasse, yielded to the last GDR mega-apartment complex in the inner city. Apartments in the "Edelplatte" (noble prefabs) were available only to select people due to their vicinity to the Wall.
Nowadays, the "Platte", predominantly in mini-format, is a favorite toy model kit or card game.

"Berlin can point to a series of periods of exemplary city construction, such as that of Friedrichstrasse in the 17th century, that of Unter den Linden in the 18th century, and to Schinkel's magnificent interventions in city construction during the 19th century. What remains to be named among the achievements of city construction in the 20th century besides Stalinallee?" (Philip Johnson, Architekt)

Reconstruction propaganda during construction on Stalinallee, 1952

Berlin during the Cold War

The Cold War was an era of bitter political, economic, and propaganda struggle between the superpowers of the USA and the Soviet Union. After victory over Hitler, the alliance between the victorious powers promptly broke down over different opinions about the political reorganization of Europe. The world was divided for decades into two power blocks, with the probably most perilous demarcation line running right through Germany and Berlin.

In February 1945, at the Yalta Conference on the Crimea, Winston Churchill, Theodor Roosevelt, and Josef Stalin had laid the foundations for post-war reorganization. Part of this agreement was the partition of Germany into four occupation zones and the repositioning of the Polish borders. Roosevelt's successor Truman clearly headed into a confrontational direction against the USSR from 1945 on. The latter was in the process of installing pro-Soviet governments across Eastern Europe. On top of this situation, on the eve of the Potsdam Conference on 16 July 1945, the USA successfully tested its first atomic bomb. This marked the beginning of a new era and a symbol of advantage over Stalin.

At Cecilienhof Palace in July 1945, the victorious powers were still able to communicate about the administration of

Churchill, Truman, and Stalin in Potsdam in July 1945

Germany as a single economic unit. Concurrently, they decided the reparations to be paid, and the de-nazification and demilitarization of Germany. Berlin, like the rest of the country, was partitioned into four occupation zones. How to put the new political structures into place produced intense quarrels among the occupation powers over the following years.

NUMBERS OF ALLIED TROOPS IN BERLIN

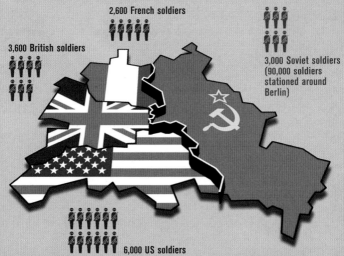

2,600 French soldiers

3,600 British soldiers

3,000 Soviet soldiers (90,000 soldiers stationed around Berlin)

6,000 US soldiers

While the three Western Allies aimed at democratic conditions, Moscow forced the "Sovietization" of East Germany step-by-step. The representatives of the USSR left the Allied Conference Council in March 1948, and in June the Allied Command Center.

After the failure of negotiations over a new self-sustaining currency – the Bear Mark (Baeren-Mark) – the Western Allies

> **"What is at stake in Berlin is not a struggle for legal rights, it is a struggle for Germany, and by extension, for Europe."**
> (US-Präsident Harry S. Truman, 1948)

decided to institute the DM as a self-sustaining currency separately in the Western zones. In reaction, Soviet officials shut the borders to their Eastern zone and decreed a blockade over West Berlin on 24 June 1948. But the city had become an important beachhead and was not to be relinquished to Soviet expansion efforts. In 1949, the creation of two German post-war countries resulted in the

Bundesrepublik Deutschland (Federal Republic of Germany) with Bonn as its capital and the Deutsche Demokratische Republik (German Democratic Republic) with East Berlin as its capital.

During the 1950s, both power blocks started energetically remilitarizing, which led to the creation of the Warsaw Pact in 1955 after the foundation of NATO in 1949. Each German government joined the opposing military alliance.

Berlin was one of the focal points of the Cold War. Together, the Americans, British, and French had about 12,200 soldiers, several dozen tanks and helicopters at their disposition. The Soviet army, by contrast, stationed 90,000 army staff in the rural surroundings of the city alone, along with thousands of fighter tanks and hundreds of jets, ready to take Berlin if necessary.

Another heavyweight central to the Cold war was intelligence activity. Berlin, an island in the middle of enemy territory, signified an ideal "eavesdropping post" for the Western Allies. The remains of the famous American listening post stand well visible to this day on the Teufelsberg hill in Grunewald.

WEST BERLIN
12,200 Western Allied soldiers
155 tanks
6 artillery cannons

To Picture Poster Inscription: All roads of
Marxism lead to Moscow Therefore CDU
CDU poster for the 1953 West German elections

The CIA and British Secret Service had
already dug a 420 m-long tunnel in 1955.
It operated under the cover name of
"Operation Gold", started at the "Site I"
facility in Rudow, reached into East Berlin
territory, and enabled them to tap telephone lines. In 1956, the ▷ KGB was
able to dismantle the project. A segment
of the tunnel is exhibited at the ▷ Allied
Museum.

After the erection of the Wall on 13 August 1961, the Cold War almost turned
into a hot one. The Soviets refused access
to East Berlin for American military trucks,
producing tanks posturing on both sides
of the Checkpoint Charly. From this Berlin
drama of military showdown, the conflict
threatened to escalate globally. The USA
was prepared to enforce their rights with
military might as they saw fit, if necessary. For several days at the end of
October 1961, American and Soviet tanks
faced each other at ▷ Checkpoint Charlie
with loaded military weaponry. NATO and
the Kremlin were in highest state of emergency, but then decided to de-escalate.
Only after the policy of détente of the
1970s, the Transit Agreement and the
German-German Foundation Agreement
did calm enter, and the situation in and
around Berlin relaxed. The end of the Cold
War was determined by President Michail
Gorbatschow's reform politics from 1985
on. East and West now cooperated and
held serious negotiations on disarmament.
Almost a year after the Wall had come
down, the GDR left the Warsaw Pact in
September 1990, which disbanded entirely
in 1991.

EAST BERLIN AND GDR
380,000 Soviet soldiers
6,900 tanks
1,200 jets

Bernauer Straße
64×65

A GDR border soldier surveys construction workers during extension works at the Wall with a loaded MP, 1962

The Berlin Wall

The two parts of Germany, and thereby of Berlin, evolved very differently after the Second World War. While the East, traditionally economically weaker, was further weakened by the Soviet occupation power taking many of its installations down and out of the country as reparations payments, the West received American aid for reconstruction. The free market also showed more flexibility than the centrally planned economy, which emphasized heavy industry and neglected consumer goods. Berlin's divided physiognomy reflected these different evolutions during the 1950s. The West Berlin center around the Kurfuerstendamm sparkled again with shops and movie theaters. By contrast, rationing and shortages, as well as mountains of rubble marked the face of many districts of East Berlin. An increasing number of people took the market and political climate in the GDR as a reason to escape to the West. 1953 alone saw more than 300,000 escapees. Because the interior German border was blocked with barbed wire and mined fields from 1952, Berlin offered one last easy escape route. One could move around freely across the four occupation zones.

The Soviet head of state Nikita Khrushchev wanted to stem the exodus tides as early as November 1958, and set a 6-month ultimatum to the Western Allies to recall their occupation troops and hand over control of access routes to the GDR. But the Western powers turned his demand down. The second Berlin crisis – after the blockade of 1948 – evolved out of this situation, with the threat of nuclear war hanging overhead. Khrushchev shunned this risk and let the ultimate date of 27 Mai 1959 pass by without consequences.

US military police at Checkpoint Charlie, 1962

The "Iron Curtain"

The refugee stream out of the GDR did not stop. Instead, it increased after the forced collectivizing of agriculture in 1960. In response, the leadership of the SED returned to a former plan for the total closure of the borders. Despite their intention, SED Party Chairman Walter Ulbricht still insisted during a press conference on 15 June 1961: "The construction workers of our city are busy mainly with the construction of apartment buildings and their work force is totally devoted to this aim. Nobody has the intention of building a wall!"

"Berlin will live, and the Wall will fall."
(Willy Brandt, 10 November 1989)

Finally, during a summit meeting in Moscow at the beginning of August, the Warsaw Pact governments agreed on closing the border between the GDR and the FRG. The Council of Ministers of the GDR followed with a decree sealing the decision. On 13 August 1961, at 01:00 a.m. of that Sunday morning, transition points were blocked and car drivers sent back by the Volkspolizei (Peoples' Police). Night owls had to find out that night by surprise that the public transport heading west was scrapped. Concurrently, heavily armed Pioneer units of the GDR started to pull up barbed wire and street barricades in the beam of headlights and to dig ditches with sand walls. At Leipziger Strasse and Potsdamer Platz, workers ripped

John F. Kennedy in West Berlin in front of the Brandenburg Gate, blocked off by the GDR government, 1963

out cobblestones and implanted concrete pillars. Machine guns were mounted. By daybreak, a total of 12,000 border police, peoples' police, and members of Factory Combat Groups took position along the sector lines. Heavy-duty surveillance at barbed wire fences now cut off the East of Berlin from the American, British, and French sectors. The fence cut right through many streets and even through graveyards.

In the USA a surprised President Kennedy was only officially briefed during the course of the morning. He expressed outrage over the barricades, but did not want to risk war over them, as long as the Soviet Union did not threaten free access to Berlin, the presence of West powers, and the freedom of the people of Berlin: **"It is not a pretty solution, but damned better than war."**

Stamp inscription:
VISIT OF THE US PRESIDENT KENNEDY
26. 6. 1963

At many points, people from East Berlin still attempted to flee to the West. They climbed down ropes let down from windows, swam across river Spree, or jumped-even including some GDR police – over the barbed wire to the other side. Three days later, workers started building the actual Wall itself.

**Achtung
Lebensgefahr
Wirkungsbereich
sowjetzonaler Minen**

Bundesgrenzschutz

Attention – Danger of Life – Effective Zone
Soviet Mines – Federal Border Guard

In the beginning it was 1.80 m tall and was additionally guarded by MG patrols and anti-tank obstacles.

Berlin's Mayor Willy Brandt and many people of West Berlin were disappointed that the USA took no action to stop the building of the Wall. In his address from Schoeneberg town hall on 17 August 1961, Brandt encouraged the 250,000 people of West Berlin and appealed to the Allies for political action. In response, Kennedy dispatched his Vice President Lyndon B. Johnson to declare his solidarity with the city. In June 1963, the US President came to West Berlin in person and assured that he himself was a Berliner at heart. Over one million people enthusiastically cheered his words.

The GDR government, by contrast, tried to block his view behind the "Iron Curtain" and covered the spaces between the columns of the Brandenburg Gate

View towards East Berlin over Leipziger Platz, through which the death strip of the Berlin Wall crossed, 1965 with huge red sheets and an immense GDR flag. To the front of those covers, they added a large propaganda poster. The Berlin Wall, just like the German internal border, grew steadily through expansion and perfection work. One generation of Wall succeeded the other. In 1975 the fourth Wall came into existence. Steel segments, 3.60 m high, were topped by smooth tubes so that thrown anchors could not hook onto the surface. Behind these lay the death strip with barbed wire blockages, electrified fences, and spring guns, with mine fields, ditches, and anti-tank obstacles, with passages for dogs and guards, and with surveillance towers. Apartment buildings close to the

The Berlin Wall in figures

Total wall length
155 km

Concrete segment wall
112 km (3–4 m high)

Metal grid fence
66 km (3–4 m hoch)

Surveillance towers
302

Surveillance shelters
20

Walking facilities for dogs
259

Guard dogs
600

Ditches blocking passage of vehicles
105 km (2,5 m deep)

Ditches for blocking tanks
0,9 km (5 m deep)

Electric signal fence
127 km

Patrol paths
124 km

Border crossings
12

Border soldiers
14,000

Successful escapes
5,075 (including **574** border soldiers)

Arrested persons
3,221

Killed refugees
190

Killed border soldiers
27

Escape tunnels
57

Mines (interior German border)
860,000

Spring guns (interior German border)
60,000

How long did the Wall exist?
28 years, 2 months, 27 days

Auction value of a Wall segment
(1990) **25,000 Euro**

The Peaceful Revolution

Wall were simply evacuated by force and torn down. Despite the elaborate installations for blocking passage, spectacular flights happened nonetheless over and over, be it through hand-made tunnels, in reconstructed disguised cars, by flying with gliders, on surfboards over the Baltic Sea, or in hot air balloons. The Museum "Haus am Checkpoint Charlie" exhibits some of the fantastic escape devices. Soon, with the first victim to die at the Wall, it became clear that people were not dealing with an **"antifascist protection wall"**, as SED propaganda would have it, but with measures which brutally forced their own population to remain in the GDR. In front of the outermost layer toward the West was a ditch to block cars from the East. Even into the spring of 1989,

escapees were still targets for sharp-shooters. Over 1,000 people lost their lives on the inner-German border, among them about 190 in Berlin alone. Thousands whose escape attempts failed were incarcerated for years. The federal government bought the freedom of about 32,000 captured and imprisoned persons from the GDR up to 1989. The price per prisoner – depending on their education – ran up to 95,000 DM. This lucrative business brought the GDR a total of about 3.5 billion DM. About the order to shoot at escapees at the Wall, Stasi head Erich Mielke is reported to have said to confidants: **"If one does shoot, one should do it in such a way that the person concerned does not get away but has to stay on our side with us. What does it bring to fire 70 bullets, and he runs to the West and they launch a huge campaign."**

Border opening at Potsdamer Platz after the fall of the Wall, 12 November 1989

As late as January 1989, Erich Honecker declared: **"The Wall will still stand in 50 or in 100 years."** But the Soviet head of state Mikhail Gorbachev declared in October of that same year: **"Life presents new challenges and we have to recognize the needs and moods of the people fast. Those who come too late will be punished by life."** Gorbatschov was to be proved right. Shortly afterwards, Honecker would find himself challenged to step down. The fall of the Wall itself then came as a surprise even to the SED leadership. A new travel decree by the GDR, which should have been publicized on 10 November 1989 only and then put into place step by step was accidentally read one day earlier, with the addition that it was activated immediately. The same night, the people of East Berlin stormed the border

GDR visa stamp from the Berlin Drewitz control point

transit points and forced the opening of the "Iron Curtain". With the people of Berlin cheering all around, demolition equipment began taking down the Wall over the following weeks. 80 grey concrete pieces found hot bidders around the world. The average price for one segment amounted to 50,000 DM. One can find a piece of the Wall in some private front yards today, whereas only a few vestiges remain in the city of Berlin itself. The inner city therefore shows markers on the ground, placed after the removal of the Wall, to indicate its former course.

"Now that which belongs together is growing together."
(Willy Brandt, 10 November 1989)

3 Rear part of the Wall at the Memorial Site "Berlin Wall"

INNER CITY DISTRICTS With the construction of the monumental workers' palaces on Stalinallee in 1952, Walter Ulbricht laid the foundation stone for the reconstruction of the capital of the GDR. About ten years later, with the construction of the Wall, any „escape from the republic" was to be hindered. From then on, barriers blocked street connections, apartment buildings, and even graveyards. Initial opposition against the GDR regime arose under the roofs of churches, the Berlin Zionskirche for one. The evening of 9 November 1989 finally brought the surprising opening of the border at Bornholmer Strasse.

1
Stadium of the World's Youth / Golf Course Sports Park
⌂ Selman Selmanagic, Reinhold Linger, 1950 → Chausseestr. 96, Map C2
Ⓤ Schwartzkopffstraße The Third World Youth Festival prompted the construction of the "Walter Ulbricht Stadium" on the grounds of the "Garde-Fuesilier-Kaserne" at Chausseestrasse from 1949 on. At the center of East Berlin, this arena offered space for up to 70,000 spectators. The simple design of the ensemble came from the Bauhaus student Selman Selmanagic and the landscape designer Reinhold Linger. Both were able to realize their ideals of modern architectural conception, right down to lamps, loud speakers, and waste paper baskets. After its inauguration in 1950, the biggest sports arena in East Berlin hosted mainly track-and-field athletic competitions, sports festivals, the annual final soccer match of the FDGB Cup, or political mass events of the SED. At the occasion of the Tenth World Festival, the arena was named "Stadium of the World's Youth". The reunified Berlin's bid to host the Olympic Summer Games 2000 led to the demolition of the arena prematurely in 1992. The bid failed, just as plans for building a mega sports hall or apartments on these grounds. Currently, this expansive area holds a public golf driving range that can be used free of charge. The German foreign intelligence service (BND – Bundesnachrichtendienst) is now preparing to construct its new high-security Berlin headquarters on the grounds of the former stadium, enabling its move from Pullach near Munich.

2
Cemetery of Wounded Veterans (Invalidenfriedhof), Remains of the Wall and Kieler Strasse Watch Tower / Memorial Guenter Litfin
⌂ 1748, 1961 → Scharnhorststr. 25, Kieler Str. 2, Map C2 Ⓢ Ⓤ Hauptbahnhof ⊕ Watch Tower: Tue–Thu 12–16, Sat 13–15 The Invalidenfriedhof (Cemetery of Wounded Veterans) with its 250-year history is among the oldest graveyards in Berlin. King Friedrich II laid its foundation in 1748 as part of the Prussian hospital for wounded soldiers. Predominantly high-ranking military of the 1813–15 Wars of Liberation found their last resting place in this cemetery. The most famous monument is Karl Friedrich Schinkel's gravesite for General Gerhard von Scharnhorst with a 6-m-high lion resting on the sarcophagus. The inclusion of the graveyard into the construction area of the Wall and into the border area started

Poster Inscription: World Festival of Youth and Students – Berlin 1973 – Capital of the GDR

the systematic destruction of nearly 2,800 graves in 1961.

The aim was to create a field of vision for surveying and shooting in the "death strip". Cast-iron crosses ended up in government-owned furnaces. On field A, soldiers built a shelter out of tombstones. Field I became a parking lot. On 24 August 1961, border patrols shot the 24-year-old Guenter Litfin in the nearby Humboldt-Hafen while he attempted to swim to the West. He was to become the first victim of the Berlin Wall. To commemorate his brother and other victims, Juergen Litfin established a little museum in the watchtower on Kieler Strasse. The tower was one of only three "leader sites", where an "arrest squadron" also had its quarters. On the Invalidenfriedhof, remains of the Wall, the patrol path, and information plaques mark the former route of the Wall. Many of the destroyed tombstones are being gradually restored, where possible.

3
Memorial "Berlin Wall"
⌂ Kohlhoff & Kohlhoff, 1998 → Bernauer Str. 111, Map D2 Ⓢ Nordbahnhof ⏱ Tue–Sun 10–17 The Memorial site "Berlin Wall" is a 70-m-long original segment of the border strip. Two 7-m-high steel walls frame the site. They render infinite reflections of the Wall on their blank, polished insides. Through slits in the back wall layer of the strip, visitors can look across the totally deserted death trip from the east, onto the guard path and the lamp posts and beyond those onto the front Wall of the strip. The neighbouring documentation center provides information on the history of the Berlin Wall. A surveillance tower offers an overview of the former course of the border along Bernauer Strasse. During the Wall's construction in 1961, numerous gravesites of the adjacent cemetery of the Sophien Church were razed to the ground without regard for their significance.

"Nobody has the inte

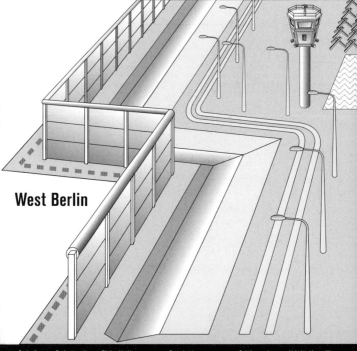

West Berlin

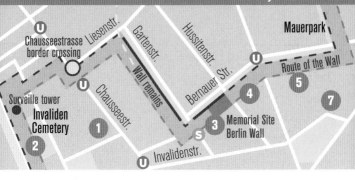

4
Reconciliation Church/
Chapel of Reconciliation

⌂ Rudolf Reitermann, Peter Sassenroth, Peter Rauch, 2000 → Bernauer Str. 4, Map D2 Ⓢ Nordbahnhof The Reconciliation Church stood at the center of the death strip of the Berlin Wall. The GDR border patrol used it as a shelter for their guards. For a free shooting range, they detonated the church in 1985. Today, the Chapel of Reconciliation stands on its exact former site, an oval limestone structure with a front made of wooden layers. These layers incorporate fragments of the ruins of the Reconciliation Church. The salvaged bells dating back to 1894 ring in front of the chapel in a separate structure.

5
Bernauer Strasse, "Tunnel 29" and "Tunnel 57"

⌂ 1962, 1964 → Bernauer Str., Map D2 Ⓤ Bernauer Straße To this day, a broad wasteland area along Bernauer Strasse separates the districts of Wedding (West)

tion to build a wall"

(Walter Ulbricht, 15 June 1961)

East Berlin

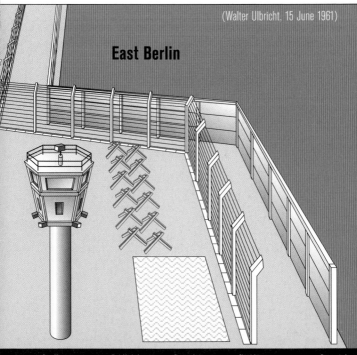

Surveillance towers   Tank blockades   Floor surface   Signal fence   Rear part of

1 Golf course at former Stadium of the World's Youth

7 Zion Church

6 Bornholmer Str. border crossing, 9 November 1989

2 Invaliden Cemetery

Kapelle der Versöhnung
Chapel of Reconciliation

4 Information stand in front of the Chapel of Reconciliation

and Mitte (East). On 15 August 1961 the legendary photograph of the Volkspolizist Conrad Schumann was taken here. He had jumped over the barbed wire fence into the West at the corner of Ruppiner Strasse. One year later, on 14 September 1962, the most spectacular mass-escape wave started in this area. The 120-m-long "Tunnel 29" between the houses Bernauer Strasse 73 (West) and Schoen-holzer Strasse 7 (East) let 29 men, women, and children escape to the West. Financed and documented by the American TV station NBC, a group of West Berlin students had dug this narrow tunnel over five months. The most successful escape happened in October 1964 through "Tunnel 57". This 143-m-long passage reached from Bernauer Strasse 97 (West) to 55, Strelitzer Strasse and allowed 57 persons to reach freedom. During to pursuit the escape helpers, the border soldier Egon Schultz was killed by a gun of one of his own comrades. The GDR cast the incident as an assassination by West Berlin agents. Today, glass pillars at the site recall the true events.

6
Border Crossing Point Bornholmer Strasse

⌂ 1961-1989 → Bösebrücke, Map D1 Ⓢ Ⓤ Gesundbrunnen **"They're going to lynch us"**, said GDR border patrols afraid on the evening of 9 November 1989 at the border crossing point Bornholmer Strasse. They meant the thousands of people storming non-stop in their direction. Shortly before, the SED Politbureau Member Guenter Schabowski had announced freedom of travel for all GDR citizens in an international press conference. He slipped by accident and said **"now, immediately"** – and that was what the people of East Berlin understood. The border soldiers knew nothing of this decree and tried desperately to obtain orders. Finally they gave in to the storm of people and stopped checking passports altogether. The people of East Berlin could travel to the West without restriction. In a briefing, the Volkspolizei said around midnight: **"All border crossing points between East and West Berlin are open."**

7
Zion Church

⌂ August Orth, 1873 → Zionskirchplatz, Map D2 Ⓤ Rosenthaler Platz Due to continuous government misinformation and press censorship in the GDR, Berlin dissidents founded the "Library of the Environment" in September 1986. The cleric Hans Simon offered them space in two basement rooms of the Zion Church. Here, they gathered literature which was difficult to acquire, organized meetings, and printed illegal flyers. On 25 November 1987, the ▷ **Stasi** stormed the rooms and arrested the activists. The vigils and protest congregations at Zion Church which followed this event unleashed protests inside and outside the country. In reaction to the Zion parishioners continuing their demonstrations with banners and protest services, the Stasi had the spire and the entrance blocked. The dissidents transferred their activities to Gethsemane Church. This was one of the first mutual campaigns by peace and human rights activists and ecological groups in the GDR.

8
Gethsemane Church

⌂ August Orth, 1893 → Stargarder Str. 77, Map E1 Ⓢ Ⓤ Schönhauser Allee The Gethsemane Church achieved far-reaching significance during the peaceful revolution of the GDR. From 2 October 1989, this church was perpetually open day and night for protest vigils and critical discussion rounds under the guiding theme **"hold vigil and pray"**. In front of the church in the light of a sea of candles, thousands of people demonstrated peacefully against the SED regime every day. On the 40th anniversary of the founding of the GDR on 7 October 1989, police and the Stasi launched an extremely brutal attack on the defenseless demonstrators with clubs and water cannons. The dissidents had been demonstrating in the center of the city – on the occasion of Mikhail Gorbachev's visit – to demand the legalization of the "New Forum". Hundreds were arrested. In March 1990, the first and only freely elected Volkskammer (Peoples' Chamber) of the GDR congregated at Gethsemane Church.

"We are the people!"

THE OPPOSITION IN THE GDR

From the end of the 1970s, as a consequence of the arms race between the two systems, the movement "Swords to Plowshares" originated in Saxony and spread over the whole GDR. Youth who carried this symbol fixed to their sleeves were banned from universities and schools. The cleric Rainer Eppelmann and regime critic Robert Havemann used the motto **"Make peace without weapons"** in 1982

In the 1980s a vast environmental movement evolved, and with the beginning of perestroika in the Soviet Union, small groups formed inside the SED calling for reform from 1985 on. The more the dissidents sought public attention, the more the surveillance machinery tightened. During the official GDR Luxemburg-Liebknecht memorial events in 1988, civil rights activists carried a banner with the Rosa Luxemburg quote **"Freedom is**

Stasi Video

Street painting

The fall of the Wall goes around the w

to demand disarmament in East and West and the right to free expression of opinion.

Illegally acquired and replicated texts or difficult-to-come-by literature were distributed under the protective roof of the protestant church. Concurrently, human rights groups sprang into life after the 1975 Helsinki Conference on security and cooperation in Europe, and demanded freedom to travel and democratic rights for the country.

always the freedom of those who think differently". The Stasi answered with arrests and deportations. A dialog with people who thought differently did not exist in the GDR.

The SED leadership sank deeper into isolation with their blockade attitude. In Poland, the reforms advanced relentlessly, Hungary opened its borders to the West. Unthinkable and unprecedented masses of people, 30,000 in number, escaped through Hungary and the Czech Republic

Neues Forum ~ Aufbruch 8

We are the People!

No Violence

The Wall must come down!

Leipzig, 25 September 1989:
1,000 men

THE MONDAY DEMOS

Under the motto "We are the people!"

Leipzig, 9 October 1989:
70,000 men

the Monday demos initiated in Leipzig had great part in the peaceful revolution

URGERBEWEGUNG "DEMOKRATIE JETZT"

in the summer of 1989 and eroded the power structures of the SED. More and more Germans, however, wanted to change the GDR from within rather than emigrate.

At the first Monday Demonstration on 4 September 1989 in Leipzig 1,000 citizens gathered and declared **"We will stay!"** The opposition groups formed political alliances step by step.

On 9/10 September, the "New Forum" sprang into life, on 12 September "Democracy Now", on 2 October the "Democratic Beginning", on 7 September a

"SWORDS TO PLOWSHARES"

and by the SED Politbureau resigning on 8 November. After the fall of the Wall on 9 November, GDR citizens occupied the

View through the Wall

German-German jubilation

Memorial site "Berlin Wall"

Social Democratic Party, and many others followed. At the Leipzig Monday Demonstration on 9 October 70,000 citizens gathered. Just seven days later, 500,000 people gathered on Alexanderplatz in Berlin and demanded freedom of expression, freedom of travel, and free elections. The peaceful revolution could not be stopped any longer. Erich Honecker's resignation on 18 October 1989 was followed on 7 November by the whole Government stepping down

first Stasi offices around the country at the beginning of December. With the founding of the Round Table on 7 December, which gave the opposition certain controls over the government, a quasi-dual government was transitionally in power. The dissolution of the Stasi was decided here. Eventually, on 18 March 1990, the first free elections in the GDR followed, from which the CDU-led "Alliance for Germany" emerged as the winner.

Demokratischer Aufbruch

"GRÜNE LIGA"

We're staying here!

Free Elections

Leipzig, 16 October 1989:
120,000 men
of the GDR. An increasing number of people came from one week to the

Leipzig, 23 October 1989:
320,000 men
next. After the fall of the Wall, the motto became **"We are one people!"**

Ostbahnhof Station
DB S U
Mühlenstr. **East Side Gallery**
FRIEDRICHSHAIN
U S
Oberbaum Bridge Stralauer Allee
border crossing
Route of the Wall
10
Köpenicker Str.
SPREE
KREUZBERG
Skalitzer Str. U
Surveillance tower
14
11

9
Friedrichshain Park
⌂ Peter Joseph Lenné, 1876, Reinhold Lingner 1945 → Am Friedrichshain, Map E2 Ⓤ Strausberger Platz Two mountains of rubble dominate Friedrichshain Park today, one 48 and the other 78 m high. Underneath lie the ruins of two immense flak shelters from the Second World War. The park held great significance for the revolutionary self-consciousness of the GDR. The victims of the street battles of the 1848 revolution, the "victims of the month of March", rest there.
On the Park's north side rises the monumental "Memorial for German and Polish Antifascists" of 1972. A 14-m-high column with the coats of arms of Poland and the GDR stands in front of the open stair area. On the other side of the park at Friedenstrasse is the "Memorial for the Inter-brigadiers of the Spanish Civil War". The statue of a freedom fighter, in a distorted posture with a sword and clenched fist, storms over a symbolic trench at the front.

10
East Side Gallery
⌂ 1961 → Mühlenstr. 47–80, Map F3 Ⓢ Ostbahnhof The East Side Gallery, between Ostbahnhof and Oberbaum-bruecke, is the longest and most famous preserved stretch of the Berlin Wall at 1.3 kilometers (back part of the former Wall toward the hinterland). Right at the river front of the Spree, shortly after the opening of the border, 118 artists from 21 countries painted this gray Wall segment. The open air gallery has stood as a listed relic of the elaborate border construction since 1992, as an impressive testament to the days of the Cold War.

Conceivably the most famous painting on the East Side Gallery is the intense brotherly kiss between Erich Honecker and the Soviet party and government head Leonid Brezhnev.

11
Surveillance Tower
Schlesischer Busch
⌂ 1963 → Puschkinallee, Map F4 Ⓢ Treptower Park As one of the only three preserved towers in the city center, this surveillance tower documents and authenticates the course of the former Wall between the districts Kreuzberg (West) and Treptow (East). It controlled the function of 18 other towers. The construction type with prefabricated concrete elements imitates that found on the Soviet-Chinese border.

12
Stalinallee / Karl-Marx-Allee
⌂ Hermann Henselmann, Hanns Hopp, Richard Paulick, Egon Hartmann, Kurt Leucht, Karl Souradny and Collective, 1952–58 → Karl-Marx-Allee, Map F3 Ⓤ Strausberger Platz Wide areas of the Friedrichshain district resembled a field of ruins after the Second World War. Among them was Grosse Frankfurter Strasse, today Karl-Marx-Strasse. The Red Army had shot its way clear with tanks and artillery when advancing from Frankfurt / Oder toward the Reichstag. On 21 December 1949, the street was renamed Stalinallee in honor of the Soviet dictator. Walter Ulbricht intended the foundation stone for the erection of Socialism in the GDR capital to lie here. Primarily and predominantly, the architect Hermann Henselmann was responsible for planning. At several segments of

10 Artsy Wall breakthrough by a Trabbi at the East Side Gallery

13 Soviet Memorial in Treptow

12 "Café Sibylle" on Karl-Marx-Allee

12 Laubengang in der Karl-Marx-Allee

12 Memorial plaques for the placement of the foundation stone at Karl-Marx-Allee

The Karl-Marx-Allee

construction over a distance of 2.3 km, "workers' palaces" arose, which were up to 300 m long, nine stories high, and which held shopping and apartment units. This metropolitan boulevard stretched from the gatehouses at Strausberger Platz to Frankfurter Tor, with expansive sidewalks and green areas. As part of the National Reconstruction Program, 45,000 people helped the construction of this "socialist street". In reaction to the increase in working norms decreed by the SED, the workers' protest at Stalinallee and at the nearby Friedrichshain Hospital escalated to a countrywide uprising of the people against the GDR regime on 16/17 June 1953. As part of de-Stalinization in 1961, the Stalinallee received its new name Karl-Marx-Allee. At the same time, during one foggy night, the 4.80-m-high Stalin monument disappeared. A piece of the Stalin statue's brass ear is visible today among other historical documents about Karl-Marx-Allee in "Café Sybille" (house no. 75). One of the demolition workers who took the brass Stalin down had preserved it and after the Wall came down he offered the piece of ear to the exhibition organizers in the "Café Sybille" as a gift.

13

Soviet Monument Treptow

⌂ 1949, Jakow Beloplski & Kollektiv → Treptower Park, Map F4 Ⓢ Treptower Park In April 1945, the Red Army had mustered 2.5 million soldiers for the battle over Berlin. 5,000 of their fallen comrades found their final resting place at the Soviet Monument in Treptow, which honors them. Ceremonies in 1946 inaugurated and dignified the memorial site as a **"symbol of victory by the glorious Soviet army over Hitler's fascism"**. The granite for its construction came largely from Adolf Hitler's demolished New Reich Chancellery. At the center of the site stands a mausoleum, from which stretches the 12-m-high brass sculpture of a Red Army soldier with his sword sunken to his feet. He stands with his boots on a smashed swastika; on his arm he carries a German child. On 31 August 1994, the Soviet army held its parting ceremony at the Treptow memorial site.

12 The Frankfurt Gate on Stalinallee, GDR postcard from the 1950s

The Berlin Airlift

Shortly before midnight on 23 June 1948, the lights went out in Berlin. Without prior warning, the Soviets had disrupted the electricity grid and were barring all access routes to the city one

consumer goods necessary for survival, daily and around the clock. Altogether, almost 200,000 flights brought around 1.5 million tons of food, fuel, and medical supplies into West Berlin. The people

15 C-54 at Columbiadamm

15 Departure hall at Tempelhof

15 Airlift Memorial

after another. Monetary reforms in the Western occupied zones preceded these events. The Soviets reacted to the introduction of the Deutschmark in the Western sectors and the intended founding of a West German government with the blockade of West Berlin. More than two million West Berlin citizens, 8,000 Allied soldiers and their 22,000 family dependents were caught in a trap. This became the hour of the US Military Governor General Lucius D. Clay. As a veteran pioneer officer and expert for re-provisioning front lines during the Second World War, he started the Berlin Airlift without hesitation, the biggest air transportation enterprise in the history of the world. From that moment on, more than 900 "raisin bombers" unloaded 13,000 tons of

of West Berlin did not have to starve to death thanks to the temerity of the pilots. Nonetheless, food supplies were rationed, and electricity was available for a few hours a day, if at all. In the Western half of the former Reich capital a frontier atmosphere developed anew. Ernst Reuter, SPD mayor (Social Democratic Party of Germany) became the symbol of the will to persist and survive. On 12 May 1949, after almost one year, Moscow lifted the blockade, realizing that the attempt at blackmail had failed. The three Western Allies did not relinquish their zones. 78 people died during this period. A memorial at ▷ **Tempelhof Airport** honors the pilots who died in accidents.

15 A "raisin bomber" prepares for landing at Tempelhof before the eyes of dozens of children

"They gave their lives for the freedom of Berlin while serving the airlift in 1948/49." (Followed by the names of pilots)

SIE GABEN IHR LEBEN FUR DIE FREIHEIT, BE
CPL. G. S. BURNS   1ST LT. C.H. KING   1ST LT. W.T. LUCAS   1ST LT. G.B.S
G   NAV/O A.J. BURTON ·F/ENG. K.A. SEABORN   CAPT. W. CUSA

14
Squatters in Kreuzberg
→ Wilhelmstr., Mariannenplatz, Cuvrystr., Map F4 Ⓤ Görlitzer Bahnhof **"Better to squat and repair than own and run down"** was the slogan of alternative groups in Kreuzberg in the late 1970s, who opposed housing speculation and sanitation through razing buildings to the ground practiced by the Berlin Senate. Whole districts with older apartment buildings were torn down to make place for anonymous concrete forts. Consequently, the citizens' initiative SO 36 occupied two empty apartments in 1979 and started renovating them. Other groups continued this form of taking action, which resulted in 160 squatted houses by 1981. The Thommy Weissbecker House on Wilhelmstrasse, the Georg von Rauch House on Marianneplatz, and the "Kerngehaeuse" (pit shell) at Cuvrystrasse were among the most famous buildings renovated by squatters. Police raids to clear the buildings of these activities provoked frequent and intense street battles and the resignation of the SPD Senate in 1981. After this followed the "Berlin line of reason" legalizing the new living situations.

15
Tempelhof Airport
🏠 Ernst Sagebiel, 1939 → Platz der Luftbrücke 1–6, Map D4 Ⓤ Platz der Luftbrücke On 8 October 1923, the first airport for public transportation opened on the Tempelhof airfield. This field had served as a military exercise ground since 1720, and from 1871 on for stationing air ships. In 1933, the airport had the highest frequency of traffic of all European airports.
On 1 Mai 1933, Adolf Hitler introduced the "Tag der Nationalen Arbeit" (Day of National Work) as a national holiday, here with a major speech in front of NSDAP and Union members. The next day, free unions were destroyed all over Germany.
Ernst Sagebiel's design of a monumental construction of the central airport came into existence from 1936–39. The airport could handle up to six million passengers per year. The 1,230-m-long flight of buildings with 284,000 square meters of gross floor space is still among the three largest buildings in the world to this day. On 28 April 1945, Soviet troops occupied the airport. In July 1945, the airport came under US army control. During the Berlin blockade, Tempelhof and the airports in Tegel and Gatow signified an important connection to various West German cities. At times, a transportation aircraft of the type Douglas "Skymaster" C-54 landed every 90 seconds with goods for West Berlin's basic survival needs. Many pilots threw sweets attached to mini parachutes from their cabins shortly before landing – thus the name "raisin bomber". The three west-pointing ribs of the Airlift Memorial recall narrow air passages. It was inaugurated in 1951 and is dedicated to the pilots who risked and lost their lives for the freedom of Berlin. At Columbiadamm on the northern edge of the Tempelhof airfield, an exhibition C-54 plane commemorates the airlift.

15 Airlift Memorial at Tempelhof Airport

S IM DIENSTE DER LUFTBRÜCKE 1948/49   CA
1ST LT. R.W. STUBER   CAPT. J.A. VAUGHN   CIV. C.V. HAGEN   PF
.TAYLOR   RAD/O. D.W. ROBERTSON   N/O. M.E. CASEY   C.APT. G. U

Willy Brandt 1913–1992

Willy Brandt was born in Luebeck on 18 December 1913 and named Herbert Frahm. In 1930, he joined the SPD Party (Social Democratic Party of Germany), switching only a year later to the Socialist Party of the Workers (SAP – Sozialistische Arbeiterpartei). After Hitler had gained power, he fought against the Nazi regime undercover as Willy Brandt from Oslo and Stockholm. His post-war political career started in 1949 as representative of the SPD in the German federal government. He became enormously popular as Mayor of Berlin (1957–66) due to his great determination. His function as foreign minister and vice chancellor in a grand coalition with the Christian Democratic Union (CDU) in 1969 led to his election as chancellor. He conducted a policy of rapprochement with Eastern European countries and marked his time in office accordingly. He fell to his knees at the Memorial of the Warsaw Ghetto Uprising, symbolically initiating a policy of détente in 1970. This policy resulted in the West German agreements with Poland and the USSR. This earned him the Nobel Peace Price in 1971. He stepped down as chancellor in 1974, due to the intelligence affair around his personal advisor Guenter Guillaume. Helmut Schmidt succeeded him in office.

On 10 November 1989, Willy Brandt pleaded for rapid German reunification in front of the Schoeneberg town hall. Brandt passed away in Unkel near Bonn on 8 October 1992. He was buried in the Waldfriedhof Postdamer Chaussee in Berlin-Zehlendorf.

16
Allied Control Council/
Court of Appeal

⌂ Paul Thoemer and Rudolf Moennich, 1909 → Elssholzstr. 30–33, Map C4
Ⓤ Kleistpark The Allied Control Council was the highest governing organ of the four occupation powers. Here, consensual and unanimous decisions were to direct Germany's affairs. Members of the Control Council on 30 July 1945 were the commanders-in-chief of each occupation power in the persons of General Eisenhower (USA), Marshal Shukov (USSR), Field Marshall Montgomery (GB), and General Lattre de Tassigny (FR). The council held its sessions at the former Court of Appeal. Under this roof, Roland Freisner had ruled the notorious People's Court (Volksgerichtshof) and sentenced opponents to the Nazi regime to death. Differences in opinion among the Western occupation powers and the Soviet Union prompted the USSR representative to leave the session of the Control Council in March 1948, which never reunited again.

"Ish bin ein Bearleener."

("I am a Berliner" The legendary sentence noted in his own phonetics by John F. Kennedy himself in 1963.)

17
Town Hall Schoeneberg
⌂ Juergensen & Bachmann, 1914
→ John-F.-Kennedy-Platz 1, Map B4
Ⓤ Rathaus Schöneberg ⊕ Mon–Sun
10–18 The Schoeneberg town hall housed the office of the Governing Mayor of West Berlin from 1949, including Ernst Reuter and Willy Brandt. Concurrently, the building was the backdrop to many great political events during the Cold War. The 70-m-high spire of the town hall has held the "Freedom Bell" financed by the USA since 1950. The radio station RIAS Berlin sent its sound far beyond the confines of Berlin. On 26 June 1963, US President John F. Kennedy visited Berlin. Facing more than 300,000 spectators, he announced his legendary words: **"All free people, wherever they live, are citizens of Berlin and, therefore, I am to be able to say as a free man proud: I am a Berliner."** The entry area of the town hall holds an interesting exhibition about Willy Brandt.

18
RIAS Berlin Building/
Deutschlandradio Kultur Building
⌂ 1948 → Hans-Rosenthal-Platz 1,
Map B4 Ⓤ Rathaus Schoeneberg
The US-funded DIAS (Drahtfunk im amerikanischen Sektor – wire communication in the American sector) went on air via the telephone network for the first time on 7 February 1946. When radio reception became equally available, the station became RIAS (Rundfunk im amerikanischen Sektor – Radio communication in the Ame-

rican Sector). From the Berlin blockade, through the peoples' uprising on 17 June, the construction of the Wall, and the Kennedy visit, to the fall of the Wall, the RIAS broadcasted objective information and critiques as "the free voice of the free world". The most famous head journalist was Egon Bahr from 1950–59, who went later held political office for the SPD. The program could reach the whole GDR – provided it went undisrupted – because it was also broadcast from Hof into the southern regions. The successor to RIAS, after a fusion with the East Berlin Deutschlandsender Kultur, is Deutschlandradio Kultur. Every day, the Freedom Bells from the Schoeneberg town hall sound the noon hour on this radio station.

19
Marlene Dietrich's Tomb
→ Friedhof Schöneberg III, Stubenrauchstr., Map A4 Ⓤ Friedrich-Wilhelm-Platz In July 1945, the soldiers of the 82nd US Airborne Division searched the destroyed city of Berlin for a certain Josefine von Losch, unofficially. She was Marlene Dietrich's mother. The famous movie star and singer had worked for the US army entertaining the troops since 1944 and had not seen her mother for many years. The Americans found the 95-year-old lady in Schoeneberg and arranged a meeting at Tempelhof Airport. Only a few

16 Statue on the former Allied Control Council

20 Kaiser Wilhelm Memorial Church

19 Marlene Dietrich's gravesite

17 Kennedy memorial plaque at Schoeneberg town hall

EINE FREIE STIMME DER FREIEN WELT

18 A FREE VOICE OF A FREE WORLD RIAS BERLIN

months later, Marlene's mother passed away. US parachute soldiers carried her to her last resting place on Schoeneberg Cemetery in the presence of her daughter. In 1960, Dietrich appeared publicly on a Berlin stage again for the first time. At the airport, her old friend Hildegard Knef, among others, welcomed her. Willy Brandt received the star warmly in the Schoeneberg town hall. The conservative media, however, could not forgive her "work for the enemy" and branded her as **"betrayer of her country".** Marlene said later on US television: **"Berlin was okay ... The audience was wonderful. The press wasn't."**

On 6 May 1992, Dietrich died in Paris. According to her last will, she was laid to rest next to her mother in Berlin. Adjacent to her, the world-renowned Berlin photographer Helmut Newton, who died in Los Angeles in 2004, found his last rest.

20
Kaiser Wilhelm Memorial Church

⌂ Franz Schwechten, 1895, Egon Eiermann, 1961 → Breitscheidplatz, Karte B3 Ⓢ Ⓤ Zoologischer Garten
The church was built in 1895 in honor of Emperor Wilhelm I. During the Second World War allied bombs destroyed the church building almost completely. The ruin of the spire remained as a "rotten tooth", and advanced to the ranks of a symbol of West Berlin. Egon Eiermann's original design for restoration after total demolition encountered protests. Finally, he expanded the ruin with a modern bell tower and church space. The facades are made of blue glass-concrete combs which fill the inside with a religiously awe-inspiring light. On 7 August 1967, Andreas Baader, Gudrun Ensslin, and others laid smoke bombs in the ruined spire in protest against the Vietnam War. On 24 December of the same year, the student leader Rudi Dutschke attempted to access the preacher stand to speak about the Vietnam War. He was intercepted by an infuriated mass attendant and beaten with a crutch until bleeding.

21
Nuclear Shelter Ku'damm Karree

⌂ 1974 → Kurfürstendamm 207–208, Map A3 Ⓤ Uhlandstraße ⌚ Mon–Sun 10–20 In 1973, in the middle of the Cold War, construction of a nuclear shelter for civil protection started deep under the parking lot of the Ku'damm Karree building. In case of emergency, 3,592 persons would have found a place for protection. Officially, it should withstand a nuclear explosion as close as 1.5 km away. Altogether, Berlin had bomb shelters for 27,000 persons. The shelter is almost intact even today. It is open to the public as part of the exhibition "The Story of Berlin".

22
Site of Benno Ohnesorg's Death

→ Bismarckstr./Krumme Str., Map A3 Ⓢ Charlottenburg On 2 June 1967, the Shah of Persia, Reza Palevi, visited Berlin. In his honor, the German Opera was to play Mozart's "Magic Flute". Human rights violations in Persia, however, had mobilized several thousand students who greeted the official visitor with paint bombs and chants of **"Shah, Shah, Charlatan"**. Presumably with monies provided by supporters of the Shah, a pro-Shah crowd trapped and attacked the demonstrators with crowbars and knuckle-dusters. The police then brutally beat the fleeing students.

Benno Ohnesorg, 27 years of age, participated in his first demonstration on that day. As he attempted to help a man at Krummestrasse, he was shot in the head and killed by Detective Sergeant Karl-Heinz Kurras. Official cover-up manipulations ensued; Kurras went to prison for only four months. After this horrible event, the students intensified their protest movements enormously, and even propagated the use of violence. One of the terrorist groups later took the name "2 June Movement", based on this event. A memorial plate and a wall sculpture at the Deutsche Oper recall the death of Benno Ohnesorg.

Rudi Dutschke 1940–1979

Rudi Dutschke spent his youth in Luckenwalde near Berlin. Early in his life, he stood up against the militarization of society in the GDR. This made studying journalism impossible – originally he wanted to become a sports journalist. Shortly before the construction of the Wall, Dutschke moved to West Berlin in 1961 to study at the Free University. He focused his interest on Marxist writings and on the history of the workers' movement. In 1966 he was elected the spokesperson for the Socialist Student Association of Germany (SDS – Sozialistischer Deutscher Studentenbund) and soon reached fame throughout the Federal Republic of Germany. In 1968, during an Anti-Vietnam-War demonstration, he publicly appealed to US soldiers to desert their army and demanded the destruction of NATO. For political opponents, Dutschke now became **"public enemy no. 1"**. On 11 April, he barely survived an attempt on his life. He had to reacquire speech and memory functions during his long therapy. After sojourns in foreign countries, Dutschke devoted his efforts to the foundation of the "Green Party". One year later, he died in the aftermath of the attempt on his life. His funeral took place on St. Annen Cemetery in Berlin.

23
Site of Rudi Dutschke's Shooting

→ Kurfürstendamm 140, Map A3

Ⓤ Adenauerplatz On 11 April 1968, the right-wing laborer Josef Bachmann fired three shots on the student leader Rudi Dutschke at 140 Kurfuerstendamm, in front of the office of the Socialist Student Association of Germany (SDS – Sozialistischer Deutscher Studentenbund). Dutschke suffered life-threatening brain damage and barely survived after three hours of surgery.

The assault happened in an atmosphere of hate campaigns against the rebellious students, campaigns which were fueled by the newspapers of the Springer conglomerate, among other media. Students throughout West Germany and the world reacted to this event with protest actions. In Berlin, demonstrators ransacked the parking lot of the ▷ **Axel Springer Publishing House** on 13 April 1968. Trucks were overthrown and set on fire. Rudi Dutschke died in 1979, only 39 years old, in Aarhus/Denmark, from the consequences of the attempt on his life.

24
Communal Living in "Kommune 1"

⌂ 1967–1969 → Stephanstr. 60, Map B2
Ⓢ Ⓤ Westhafen Members of the
Socialist Student Association of Germany
(SDS – Sozialistischer Deutscher Studentenbund) united in the first politically
motivated commune in Germany in West
Berlin from 1 January 1967. In reaction
to the conservative moral attitude of the
1960s, a principle of living was pursued
which embraced freedom from financial
security, ownership, private sphere, or
performance pressure, but which was
instead based on enjoyment and motiva-
tion. They used the studio of the uninitia-
ted writer Uwe Johnson at 14 Niedstrasse
in Berlin Friedenau for their first living
quarters while he sojourned in the USA.
The first commune members (communards) included Dieter Kunzelmann, Fritz
Teufel, Ulrich Enzensberger, Dagmar
Seehuber, Dorothea Ridder, Volker Gebbert,
and Rainer Langhans.
Obtrusive actions, like the planned "pud-
ding attack" on the US Vice President
earned them the status of pop stars.

Pin of the anti-Springer demonstrators, 1968

After the Shah's visit, Fritz Teufel was
even incarcerated for a short while in
Moabit remand prison. Springer headlines
read exclusively **"horror communards"**.
In the summer of 1968, "Kommune 1"
moved into an empty factory on Stephan-
strasse in Moabit. Now sex, music, and
drugs entered the agenda, as did the
photo model Uschi Obermaier who had
moved in. At the end of 1969, the Berlin
commune slowly fell apart. Obermaier
and Langhans went to Munich. The year
1981 witnessed the foundation of the
"Chaos Computer Club" in the former
rooms of the "Kommune 1".

23 Devastated parking lot of the Springer Publishing House after the assault on Dutschke's life, 13 April 1968

OUTER DISTRICTS AND SURROUNDING AREA In the Allied occupation zones of Berlin, each victorious government had its own military headquarters. These were self-contained city districts with military quarters and establishments for army families, typical in style for their country. Soviet intelligence additionally maintained special camps and prisons, which were later run by the Stasi, such as the one at Hohenschoenhausen. They figured on no map. Their history was revealed only after German reunification.

1
Soviet War Memorial Schoenholzer Heide

⌂ Kolektiv Konstantin A. Solowjew, 1949 → Germanenstr., Volkspark Schönholzer Hiede, Map C2 Ⓢ Wilhelmsruh After 1947, the third Soviet war memorial in Berlin was built at the Schoenholzer Heide park. On the monumental grounds, 13,200 officers and soldiers of the Red Army, victims of war, found their last resting place. 16 chambers for sarcophagi flanked the way to a centrally oriented 33.5-m-high obelisk. In front of it stands the sculpture "Mother Earth", grieving for her son killed in action.

2
Castle Niederschoenhausen and SED Residential Area Pankow

⌂ Johann Friedrich Eosander, 1664 → Ossietzkystr. Majakowskiring, Map C2 Ⓢ Ⓤ Pankow **"Pardon me; is this the special train to Pankow? I just have to get there, just to get to East Berlin."** These were the lyrics of Udo Lindenberg's 1983 song. The rock star addressed Erich Honecker directly with his song, to ask for the opportunity to perform publicly in the GDR. The **"special train to Pankow"** reached its destination. On 25 October 1984, Lindenberg gave a concert at the Palace of the Republic. His song, so famous in the GDR, was not permitted, however, and he never got to Pankow either. Strictly guarded from the public, leading party elite of the GDR lived there from 1945 to 1960:
- **Walter Ulbricht** (General Secretary of the SED Central Committee) – Majakowskiring 28
- **Wilhelm Pieck** (first President of the GDR – Majakowskiring 29

- **Otto Grotewohl** (first head of government of the GDR – Majakowskiring 46/48
- **Erich Honecker** (General Secretary of the ZK of the SED) – Majakowskiring 58
- **Erich Mielke** (Minister for State Security of the GDR – Stille Strasse 10
- **Markus Wolf** (head of GDR foreign intelligence – Rudolf-Ditzen-Weg 18/20

At Majakowskiring 34, Minister of Culture Johannes R. Becher wrote the text for the national anthem of the GDR in 1949, composed by Hans Eisler. **"Resurrected from ruins / looking to the future / let us serve your good / Germany, united fatherland ..."**
After Honecker gained power in 1971, only the instrumental interpretation of the anthem was permitted from then on. The GDR leadership no longer aspired for a "united fatherland".
Fearing a people's uprising similar to Hungary in 1956, the highest party leaders moved from Pankow to Wandlitz, which was a more secure urban forest district outside Berlin. The castle of Niederschoenhausen in Pankow was the office of the GDR President from 1949–60, then a government guesthouse. During the years 1989/90, the "Round Table" assembled here for negotiations about transformations of the GDR.

3
Mies van der Rohe House
⌂ Mies van der Rohe, 1932 → Ober-
seestr. 60, Map C2 ⏲ Tue–Fri 13–18,
Sat–Sun 14–18 **"But that is a weird
house."** Erich Mielke, the Minister for
State Security, is reported to have said
during the 1950s. He meant a one-storey
building of brick stone under a flat roof,
conceived in 1932 by the Architect
Mies van der Rohe for Mr and Mrs Lemke
in Berlin-Weissensee. After the Second
World War, the Soviet army ran down the
building, using it as a storehouse and
parking garage. Agents and members of
the Stasi predominantly moved into the
neighborhood. Nobody recognized the
architectural significance of the building.
In 1951, a Stasi officer had the totally
dilapidated house renovated for himself
and his family, thereby saving it from
demolition. Today, the Mies van der Rohe
House is back in its original condition and
serves as an exhibition site for modern art.

4
Robert Havemann House
→ Burgwallstr. 4, Grünheide, Map D3
Along with Wolf Biermann, Professor
Robert Havemann was one of the most
prominent regime critics of the GDR.
Following a critical lecture series at the
Emil Fischer Auditorium of the Humboldt
University, he was excluded from the SED
and later even barred from carrying out
his profession. Of all people, Havemann,
the antifascist par excellence, was the
man whom the Stasi attempted to dis-
credit, and with all its might. But this
man's upright and pacifist intellectual
standing then increasingly became an
ideal for many opponents in the GDR.
To censure Havemann even more, the
Stasi put him under house arrest from
1976–79. His home in Gruenheide, his
family, and his friends were surveyed
around the clock. In 1982, he attempted
to organize a general German Peace
movement together with the Pastor
Eppelmann ("Berliner Appell"). He died
that very same year. During the fall of
1989, the largest civil rights movement
in the GDR, the "New Forum", was founded at his house.

5
Memorial Site for Socialists
⌂ Mies van der Rohe, 1926, Wilhelm
Pieck, 1951 → Gudrunstr., Map D3
Ⓢ Ⓤ Lichtenberg In the night from
15 to 16 January 1919, the founders of
the KPD (Communist Party of Germany)
Rosa Luxemburg and Karl Liebknecht
were murdered in the Tiergarten Park.
The city accorded the communists a final
resting place in the "criminal corner" of
the Friedrichsfelde Central Cemetery. The
architect Mies van der Rohe created a
memorial in their honor in 1926, which
the Nazis destroyed in 1935. Wilhelm
Pieck, the first president of the GDR,
conceived a "Memorial Site for Socialists"
for the main entrance of the cemetery in
1951. Next to a centrally aligned stone
with the inscription "Die Toten mahnen
uns" (the dead appeal to our conscious-
ness), are the graves of Ernst Thaelmann,
Rosa Luxemburg, Karl Liebknecht, Otto
Grotewohl, and Walter Ulbricht. Every
year, on the second weekend in January,
a memorial ceremony takes place at this
site. In 1988, when civil rights supporters
wanted to use Rosa Luxemburg's ideas
for the good of the GDR, they were
arrested for carrying a banner reading:
**"Freedom is always the freedom of those
who think differently."**

6
**Ministry for State Security/
Research and Memorial Site
Normannenstrasse**
⌂ 1963 → Ruschestr. 103, "Haus 1",
Map C3 Ⓤ Magdalenenstraße
⏲ Mon–Fri 11–18, Sat–Sun 14–18
From the time of the founding of the
Ministry for State Security (MfS-Minis-
terium fuer Staatssicherheit) in 1950,
GDR intelligence had its headquarters in
Normannen-/Magdalenenstrasse in Berlin
Lichtenberg. During the following years,
the Stasi spread over the whole district.
In "Haus 1" was the office of the Chief
of Intelligence, Erich Mielke. His work
and private space, his meeting auditorium, and yes, even kitchen and bathroom
are preserved in their original state from
the 1950s. On the other floors, an exhibition informs visitors about the history

3 Mies van der Rohe House

1 Soviet Memorial Schoenholzer Heide

6 Former Ministry for State Security

6 Mielke's living room and bathroom

7 Entry gate to the former Stasi prison

7 Erich Honecker's portrait in a Stasi interrogation room

The Stasi

On 8 February 1950, the Ministry for State Security of the GDR (MfS – Ministerium fuer Staatssicherheit) was founded under the leadership of Wilhelm Zaisser. As an intelligence service, the MfS fell was opened, and millions of documents were established about individuals' personal lives. For defectors or escape helpers, the MfS shunned no means, including assassination and kidnapping. For "Day X", if another uprising by the people of the GDR should happen, the MfS had planned "isolation camps" all

7 "Tiger cage"

7 Single cell

7 Cell doors

under the authority of the SED and saw itself in the role of **"sword and shield of the party"**. Its main duties were

- Surveillance of all societal aspects of life and combating opponents of the regime
- Intelligence activities through spying and anti-espionage measures
- Investigation of political criminals and security detention of enemies of the government.

For these duties, the MfS occupied about 91,000 fulltime employees in 1989. Guenter Guillaume was one of them, who worked in the office of Willy Brandt as a spy. Additionally, the MfS had 175,000 unofficial coworkers (IM – Inoffizielle Mitarbeiter). The full extent of spying activities only was revealed after the fall of the Wall. Telephones were tapped, mail over the country. In the Augustusburg near Chemnitz alone, 6,000 people could have been placed in detention. Despite all this, the Stasi failed in suppressing opposition movements. The occupation of Stasi offices by civilian movements resulted in the decision to disband the MfS on 14 December 1989.

Erich Mielke 1907–2000

Erich Mielke grew up in a working-class family in Berlin Wedding. He worked on as journalist for the communist party newspaper "Rote Fahne" and for the KPD's self-defense section from 1928. After the assassination of two police officers he fled to the USSR, where he received military and political training at the "Lenin-School". From 1936–39 he fought in the Spanish Civil War. After the Second World War he worked his way up through the ranks of the police to the Stasi, which he helped establish from 1950 on. He ascended to become one of the most powerful men of the GDR when he was nominated Minister for State Security in 1957. He remained one of the hardliners. After the reunification of Germany, a court sentenced him to six years in prison, in relation to the murder of the policemen in 1931. For health reasons, Mielke was released in 1995 before completion of his sentence. He died in 2000 in a senior citizen home in Berlin.

of the Stasi and the opposition in the GDR. In the weeks after the opening of the Wall, the Stasi carried on its activities unabashed and destroyed many documents. On 15 January 1990, about 10,000 demonstrators occupied the Stasi headquarters and put an end to the annihilation of documents. "Haus 7" now houses the archive of Stasi documentation, with about 6 million person-related documents. Anyone spied on by the Stasi during GDR times can gain access to the relevant documents through the official administration in charge.

7
Ministry of State Security Remand Prison/Memorial Site Berlin Hohenschoenhausen

⌂ 1961 → Genslerstr. 66, Map D2
⏱ Mon–Sun 9–18, guided tours Mon–Fri 11, 13, Sat–Sun 10–16 (start every hour) After the Red Army's victory over Berlin, the Soviet Military Administration (SMAD) established a special camp in what was a former canteen in the Hohenschoenhausen district. Without hearings by a court, German citizens suspected of being Nazis or opponents to the occupation policy were interned in this camp. Up to 4,200 prisoners were

crammed into tiny quarters and suffered from cold, hunger, and illness. Estimates hold that about 3,000 people died in this camp until it was disbanded in 1946. The remaining people were transferred to the ▷ **Soviet Special Camps** in Oranienburg. The premises in Hohenschoenhausen now served the SMAD as a remand prison. Many were immediately convicted here to 10 and up to 25 years of forced labor, and deported to the Soviet GULAGs.

In 1951, the ▷ **Ministry for State Security** (MfS) took the institution over. The infamous "U-Boot" in the humid, cold basement cells was continued by the Stasi. Prisoners were brutally tortured in this basement and kept in isolation for weeks. Up to 1962, the MfS oversaw construction of an additional labor camp, a new prison building with 200 cells, interrogation rooms, and a hospital. In the 1960s and 70s, Hohenschoenhausen predominantly witnessed the incarceration of critics of the regime and of potential refugees suspected of trying to escape from the GDR. The prisoners were kept in the dark for the length of their incarceration, and few prisoners knew where they were at all. Communication with other prisoners and prison guards was prohibited. The only contact person was the interrogation office. How many people passed through this institution is unknown to this day.

SINGLE CELL IN THE STASI PRISON

1. wooden bed with flat mattress
2. wooden table and stool
3. "Window" made of glass construction stones
4. toilet, faucet, and mirror
5. door with hatch and spyhole

16185

8 Soviet Military Administration Berlin Karlshorst, 1945

9 Bunker ruins at Wuensdorf

9 Lenin Statue at Wuensdorf

9 Special bunker at Wuensdorf

9 Ulbricht, Marshall Jakubowski, and the Soviet Ambassador Abrassimov in Wuensdorf, 1963

Wuensdorf or "Wjunsdorf"

On 9 October 1990, almost one year after the opening of the Wall, the prison was closed. The spartan interior with its foul-smelling linoleum floor has survived time unaltered until today. During guided tours through this memorial site, former prisoners give visitors impressive accounts about the gruesome typical day in prison.

8
Soviet Military Administration, KGB Headquarters / German-Russian Museum Berlin Karlshorst

⌂ 1938, 1930 → Zwieseler Str. 4, Köpenicker Allee 39–57, Map D3 Ⓢ Karlshorst ⏲ Tue–Sun 10–18

On 3 May 1945, the Red Army marched into Berlin Karlshorst and occupied the apartment houses of about 8,000 people without further ado. A former German military academy on Zwieseler Strasse served the Soviet Military Administration (SMAD) under Marshal Georgi K. Shukov as headquarters. Five days later, Wilhelm Keitel, General Field Marshall, ratified the unconditional surrender of the German military and thereby the end of the war in Europe here with his signature. From 1967, the house served as a **"museum for the unconditional surrender of fascist Germany during the Great Patriotic War of 1941–1945"**. The revised version of the exhibition is now part of the German-Russian Museum and documents in detail the course of the war of total annihilation against the Soviet Union. Until 1963, half of the district of Karlshorst was sealed off. The Military Barracks No. 1 for the Berlin Brigade of the Soviet Army stood on Treskowallee. The former St. Antonius Hospital on Koepenicker Allee became the German headquarters of the KGB. This was the biggest foreign division of the Soviet intelligence service. About 1,000 employees were busy here with the preparation of agents for espionage activity in the West.

9
High Command of the Soviet Troops / Wuensdorf Book Town

⌂ 1938 → Wünsdorf, Gutenbergstr. 9, Map C4 ⏲ Mon–Fri, 14–16, Sat–Sun 11–17, Garrison Museum Mo–Fr 13–17, Sa–So 11–17 The small village of Wuensdorf, 50 km south of Berlin, was the headquarters of the command of the German military during the Second World War. The giant premises with underground shelters for intelligence, shelters with living quarters, a jet fleet, military quarters, and a field for military exercise fell into the hands of the Red Army unscathed in April 1945. As seat of the Soviet High Command in the GDR, Wuensdorf evolved into one the most important strategic sites and one of the largest for stationing military of the Soviet bloc. The whole area became Soviet territory. At times, up to 60,000 military dependents had their domicile here. A direct railway and daily trains connected "Wjunsdorf" with Moscow. In case of war, the totality of strategic decision-making for the GDR was planned to be transferred to the Soviet High Command. In such a case, "Wjunsdorf" would have become the center of power instead of East Berlin. Today, the village is a peace-loving book town with countless second-hand bookstores. The Garrison Museum documents the history of the former military command station. Guided tours through the shelters are also available to visitors.

Lucius D. Clay 1897–1978

Lucius Dubignon Clay was born in the USA on 23 April 1897, as the son of the Senator of the State of Georgia. As a graduate of the West Point Military Academy, he entered the Army Engineering Corps. Following the Allied invasion of Normandy, Clay organized the rapid restoration of the Port of Cherbourg as deputy to General Dwight D. Eisenhower. Shortly before the end of the Second World War, Clay became Deputy Chief in Command of the US occupation troops in Germany. In his role as Military Governor of the American occupation zone and in command of the US Field Army in Europe, Clay expedited the democratization of Germany from 1947 on, and defended it against the high demolition demands coming from the USSR. He decisively opposed the Berlin blockade and initiated the Berlin Airlift without hesitation. Clay's belief that a retreat from the city would have unforeseeable consequences secured the enduring freedom of West Berlin. Four-Star General Clay retired from the army in 1949. One year later he handed the people of West Berlin the "Freedom Bell". Berlin appointed Clay its Honorary Citizen in 1965. He received the Grand Cross of the Order of Merit of the Federal Republic of Germany. He passed away at the age of 81 in 1978.

10
Andrews Barracks / Federal Archives

⌂ Fleischinger & Voigtal, 1878 → Finckensteinallee 63, Map B3 Ⓢ Lichterfelde-West When the US Army took over the military grounds at Finckensteinalle in Berlin-Lichterfelde from the Red Army in a ceremony in July 1945, the main building still carried the inscription "Body Guard Adolf Hitler" (Leibstandarte). The elite units of the armed forces of the SS (Waffen SS) had their headquarters here until 1945. Under US administration, the military buildings were called Andrews Barracks and served the military police, the 298th Army Band, various divisions, and as habitation for the last infantry division made up exclusively of Afro-American soldiers. The other big military barracks of the "US Berlin Brigade" were the McNair Barracks in the former Telefunken factory in Lichterfelde, the Turner Barracks of the armored divisions in Dahlem, as well as the Roosevelt Barracks in Steglitz. Since 1995, the Federal Archives of the Parties and of Mass Organizations of the GDR have been housed on the grounds of the Andrews Barracks.

11
General Lucius D. Clay Headquarters / Consulate General of the USA

⌂ 1939 → Clayallee / Saargemünder Str., Map B3 Ⓤ Oskar-Helene-Heim The greatest contingent of the Western Allies in Berlin consisted of the US Army with 6,000 soldiers and stationed at the General Lucius D. Clay Headquarters. From July 1945, these headquarters were located at the building of the former Regional Division of the Aviation Command III in Zehlendorf. The City Commander General Lucius D. Clay also had his office on these premises, along with parts of the US Embassy. From here, Clay commanded not only the American occupation zones in Germany but also the airlift during the Soviet blockade of Berlin in 1948.

After the construction of the Wall, the American troops contingent was officially named the **"Berlin Brigade"**. Surrounding

The "Berlin-Brigade"

the headquarters, the US Army maintained its own infrastructure with apartment buildings, schools, libraries, and a shopping center at Truman Plaza, swimming pools, and movie theaters. At Saargemuender Strasse, the army media station AFN (American Forces Network) provided radio and television entertainment just like home. After German reunification, the "Berlin Brigade" had achieved its mission and was disbanded by US President Bill Clinton in 1994. The Consulate General at Clayallee 170 will remain there until completion of its new premises at Pariser Platz.

"Defenders of Freedom" patch of the "Berlin Brigade"

12
Allied Museum

→ Clayallee 135, Map B3 Ⓤ Oskar-Helene-Heim ⏰ Tue–Sun 10–18 How foes change into friends is illustrated in the Allies Museum. The permanent exhibition has been under the roof of the former US Army movie theater "Outpost" and the Major Arthur D. Nicholson Memorial Library since 1994. The exhibition honors the engagement of the three Western powers in Berlin and West Germany. Among the many thousand exhibits are the last control house of ▷ **Checkpoint Charlie**, a "Raisin Bomber", army Jeeps, a spy tunnel from the Cold War and a surveillance tower with a piece of the Berlin Wall.

13
Field Station Berlin Teufelsberg

⌂ US Army 1964 → Teufelsseechaussee, Teufelsberg, Map B3 After twelve years of Nazi dictatorship and six years of war, the highest point of Berlin soon became a 120-m-high mountain of rubble made of ruins of bombed houses. Originally, this ground held the empty buildings of the Military Technical University planned in the "Third Reich", including extensive air raid shelters. When demolition through detonation failed, the whole area was simply filled with rubble. Since 1951, the US Army and the National Security

12 Part of a CIA spy tunnel which reached into East Berlin

15 Apartment unit "Type Berlin"

15 Entrance to the apartment unit (Corbusier House)

15 Foyer of Corbusier House

14 Olympic bell in front of the British headquarters

14 British parade at Olympic Stadium, 1964

16 Allied prison for war criminals, 1982

Agency (NSA) used "Site 3" on the Teufelsberg to tap into the Eastern Bloc's telephone communication. The East German intelligence service, however, managed to place a mole at the site. The white domes of the antenna towers are still visible from far away, even after the dismantling of the station. In winter, the Teufelsberg provides Berlin with the best ski facilities. It even once hosted a world cup competition.

14
British Army Headquarters/ Olympia Field

⌂ Werner March, 1936 → Friedrich-Friesen-Allee, Map B3 Ⓢ Olympiastadion (Ost) ⏲ Wed–Sun 10–18 Immediately after the Second World War, the headquarters of the British occupying army moved into the facilities, which were built 1936 as the Reich Sports Field at the Olympic Stadium. The domed hall of the "House of German Sport" had hosted the fencing competitions of the summer Olympic Games. Now it housed the offices of the British military commander. Cricket and rugby games were now enjoyed on the surrounding green areas. The May Field, once a Nazi parade ground with space for up to 400,000 people, was now used for polo tournaments and concerts. The buildings housing the military spread along the length of Heerstrasse, in Spandau and around the Montgomery Military Barracks in Kladow. A cemetery for British soldiers also borders Heerstrasse.

Since the British troops left in 1994, the "Haus des Deutschen Sports" has held a museum with the history of the Olympic premises. The Olympic Stadium and the surrounding training grounds are the home of the Hertha BSC soccer club.

15
Unit for Living "Berlin Type" (Unité d'habitation "Typ Berlin")

⌂ Le Corbusier, 1958 → Flatowallee 16, Map B3 Ⓢ Olympiastadion As part of the International Construction Show InterBau, which took place in West Berlin in 1957, the world-renowned Swiss Architect Le Corbusier made a revolutionary

contribution to the construction of living spaces in the aftermath of the war. At the edge of the Olympic Stadium, he built a unit for living (Unité d'habitation) in the previous style realized in Marseille and Nantes. Like a vertical city, the gigantic unit rises 53 m high and stretches 141 m long out of a forest and residential area in Charlottenburg. The 530 apartments, mostly arranged as maisonettes, are accessible through interior roads (rues intérieures), which are over 130 m long. The entry hall with a post office and a shop can also serve as a meeting area, and so can the communal facilities on the roof.

16
Allied Prison for War Criminals Berlin Spandau/Spandau Shopping Center

⌂ 1878 → Wilhelmstr. 23, Map B3 Ⓢ Spandau After the Nuremberg Trials of the main war criminals on 18 July 1947, seven of the convicted Nazi politicians and military commanders arrived in Berlin-Spandau to serve their time in prison according to their sentence:

- **Life sentence** – Rudolf Hess, Walter Funk, Erich Raeder
- **20 years** – Baldur von Schirach, Albert Speer
- **15 years** – Constantin von Neurath
- **10 years** – Karl Doenitz

The Allies had selected the prison especially for this purpose. The four occupation powers shared the duties of guarding the prison in a monthly rhythm. Speer ran 49 rounds on the prison grounds every day to keep busy, imagining he was running around the world. By the day of his release, he had accumulated 31,000 km. Additionally, he secretly wrote his memoires and the "Spandau Diaries" on over 20,000 sheets of paper-both later became bestsellers. After premature releases, the Fuehrer's deputy Rudolf Hess was the last prisoner in 1966. Petitions for mercy failed due to a Soviet veto. On 17 August 1987, at the age of 93, he committed suicide. The very same year, the prison was torn down. A shopping center now stands in its place.

The Reign of the Victors

"We demand peace!": Soviet propaganda poster for the Potsdam Conference, 1945

17
RAF Airport Gatow/Air Force Museum of the Armed Forces of the Federal Republic of Germany
⌂ 1935 → Kladower Damm 182–188, Map A3 ⊙Tue–Sun 9–17 In July 1945, the British Royal Air Force (RAF) took over Gatow Airport from the Red Army. During the Soviet blockade of Berlin, this little airport became the most important transfer site for the airlift. On the nearby Havel river, "salt transporters" landed, airboats of the type "Sunderland". Today, the airport predominantly serves as the Air Force Museum. More than 100 years of aviation history are on show, from the Rumpler-Taube of 1910 to modern turbo jets.

18
KGB Prison Potsdam/Memorial Site KGB Prison Potsdam, Amnesty International
⌂ 1918 → Leistikowstr. 1, Map A4 ⊙ May till October, Sat–Sun 11–17 The suburb of Nauen is one of the prettiest residential areas in Potsdam. A few steps away from Cecilienhof palace, among detached houses restored with much care and love, one suddenly faces a sad deteriorated building with windows and doors behind iron bars-the former KGB prison of Potsdam.

For more than half a century, this area was Soviet prohibited territory surrounded by a 2-m-high wall and surveillance towers. In August 1945, the Soviet anti-espionage section occupied the villa of the "Protestant Church Aid Association" and transformed it into a prison. The KGB incarcerated mainly unlawfully arrested German youth here, and from 1955 on exclusively members of their own army. From the darkened basement cells, many were deported to Soviet GULAGs for forced labor. In 1994, the KGB cleared the premises, hermetically sealed until then.

The traces of the gruesome process of incarceration are preserved virtually unaltered. A permanent exhibition in the former prison cells documents the history of the house and its people.

19 For the Potsdam Conference, a red star made of flowers was planted in the courtyard of the Cecilienhof Palace

19
Cecilienhof Palace
⌂ Paul Schulze-Naumburg, 1917
→ Im Neuen Garten, Potsdam, Map A4
Ⓢ Potsdam Hauptbahnhof ⊙ Tue–Sun
9–17 After the Second World War, on
17 July 1945, the victorious powers
convened the Potsdam Conference at
Cecilienhof Palace to discuss the destiny
of Germany in a reorganized Europe. The
host Josef Stalin (USSR) received Harry
S. Truman (USA) and Winston Churchill
represented by Clement A. Attlee (Great
Britain) at the round table of the Great
Hall. Germany was to be democratized
and de-nazified. The principles laid down
in the "Potsdam Agreement", however,
were interpreted differently by the different participants, a fact which ultimately
led to the division of Germany in the
Cold War. The conference room and the
relevant offices at Cecilienhof Palace
are now a memorial site.

20
Stasi Remand Prison Potsdam /
Memorial Site Lindenstrasse 54
⌂ 1737, 1909 → Lindenstr. 54/55,
Map A4 Ⓢ Potsdam Hauptbahnhof
⊙ Tue, Thu, Sat 9–17
From 1817 on, this baroque City Palace
in the heart of Potsdam served as the
city's court of justice. During the years
1909/10, a 5-storey prison annex was
built on the rear side with 54 cells for
90 prisoners. The Nazis incarcerated
regime critics here. The Senate of the
"People's Court" (Volksgerichtshof)
assembled in the front part and convicted
many people to many years of punish-
ment in high-security prisons or to
death. The "Court for Genetic Health",
which also had its seat here, decreed
hundreds of forced sterilizations. After
the war, the building served the Soviet
intelligence service NKWD as a remand
prison until 1952. After that, the Stasi
took over the prison on these premises.
Colloquially, people called the building
the **"Lindenhotel"**. The last prisoners were
set free here on 11 November 1989.
Today a memorial site in these historical
rooms commemorates more than 50 years
of political terror.

The KGB

Komitet Gosudarstvennoi Besopasnosti,
KGB for short, was the "Committee
for State Security", that is the Soviet
intelligence service. It emerged from
the Interior Intelligence NKWD and
the Ministry of the Interior MWD
in 1954. Its main mission consisted
of foreign intelligence as well as the
surveillance and liquidation of opponents to the USSR regime. As
appendage to the Red Army, the KGB
followed it into Germany to persecute
Nazis. Prisons and ▷ **Soviet Special
Camps**, often with randomly interned
civilians, soon covered the whole
Soviet occupation zone. Thousands
of Germans were deported from here
into labor camps in the USSR. In
Berlin Karlshorst, the KGB also had its
largest foreign branch. ▷ **Cecilienhof
Palace** in Potsdam served as the
headquarters of the representative
of the anti-espionage division.
The KGB was disbanded on 6 November 1991. The Federal Security
Service (FSB) took over its duties.
A KGB officer with the cover name
of "Platow" later came to fame as
Russia's President Vladimir Putin.
He owes his good command of the
German language to his five years
of service as an agent in Dresden.

KGB symbol

21
Border Crossing Point Glienicker Bridge

⌂ Johann Caspar Harkort, 1907, 1949
→ Potsdamer Chaussee, Map A4

At daybreak on 10 February 1962 at 08:44 a.m. precisely, Francis Gary Powers crossed the white border demarcation in the middle of the Glienicker Bridge from East to West. Nearly two years before, the US pilot had been shot down in his "U2" plane during his reconnaissance flight over the Soviet Union. Now the CIA exchanged him for the high KGB Officer Ivanovitch Abel caught in the USA.

The Allies used this bridge for further intelligence maneuvers later on. So it was on 11 June 1985, at 12:00 p.m., when the biggest exchange of intelligence agents during the Cold War took place. Four Eastern agents were exchanged for 25 CIA spies detected in the GDR. A West German TV crew filmed the "police story". The last swap of intelligence workers occurred here in February 1986.

Since the fall of the Wall, this world-renowned bridge at the outermost southwestern edge of Berlin has been free to passage.

22
Border Checkpoint Dreilinden Drewitz, Checkpoint Bravo

⌂ 1961–1989 → A 115, exit Zehlendorf, Map B4 Ⓢ Wannsee Germans who took the transit stretch on Highway A2 to reach the border crossing Dreilinden, that is Checkpoint Bravo at Helmstedt, exposed themselves to long waiting times, picky interrogations and intensive controls by GDR border administrators. To the side stood a memorial with a Soviet T34 tank, which had supposedly been the first to reach Berlin in 1945. The Soviet army took the tank down when it left in 1990. Since then a pink snow plow has decorated the stand. Some buildings of the border crossing are still preserved, along with a command tower at Stahnsdorfer Damm, which is planned to be made into a memorial site.

23
Graves of Ernst Reuter and Willy Brandt

→ Potsdamer Chaussee 75–77, Map B4
Ⓢ Schlachtensee When Berlin's mayor Ernst Reuter died in his home on Buelowstrasse from the consequences of a flu infection on 29 September 1953, thousands of citizens spontaneously placed candles in their windows. Over one million people bade him farewell at his funeral on the Zehlendorf Waldfriedhof on Potsdamer Chaussee. In the adjacent tomb of honor, the former mayor of West Berlin and chancellor Willy Brandt found his last resting place on 8 October 1992. He influenced the history of Berlin in the 20th Century by peaceful means as few others did. A memorial plaque at the Berlin home of the Brandt family at 14 Marinesteig in Dahlem honors his merits.

24
Marienfelde Emergency Camp / Marienfelde Memorial Site Emergency Camp

⌂ 1953 → Marienfelder Allee 66–80, Map C4 Ⓢ Marienfelde ⏱ Tue–Sun 10–18 After the division of Germany and Berlin into four occupation zones and until the construction of the Wall in 1961, thousands of people fled every month to the Western sectors. Berlin, above all, was the eye of the needle into freedom, which prompted the opening of the Marienfelde Emergency Camp in April 1953. Until German reunification in 1990, it was the first place for seeking contact for about 1.35 million refugees who had managed to escape the GDR. Here, these people were greeted with initial assistance, items of daily necessity, and shelter. After interrogation by the Western Allies' and West Germans' intelligence officers, most of them could fly on to West Germany.

A permanent exhibition about the German-German escape movement impressively renders the history of this emergency camp, including an original room exactly as it sheltered refugees in the 1950s.

21 Exchange of agents on Glienecker Bridge, 1986

18 Former KGB prison, Potsdam

18 Cell entrance at the former KGB prison

18 Prisoner toilets in the bathroom

24 Exhibition room at Marienfelde

22 Soldiers of the Allied victorious powers at Checkpoint Bravo, 1948

The Soviet Special Camps

With the advance of the Allied troops, numerous prison camps arose on German territory for the transitory internment of members of the German armed forces and Nazi officials. In the Soviet occupation zone, ten "Special Camps" were erected from 18 April 1945 on. Many oners were convicted according to lawful procedures. Among the convicted were often innocent civilians and even persons under legal age limits.

In 1946, 27,500 German prisoners were to be deported to mines in Siberia as part of reparation payments and were to

29 Entry to the memorial site   29 GDR Sculpture in Sachsenhausen   29 Brick barracks of Zone II

prisons, high-security penitentiary, and basement incarceration sites were added, which fell under the control of the Soviet intelligence service NKWD. Additionally, there was Camp No. 69 in Frankfurt/ Oder, for German prisoners of war who were to be deported to the USSR. Contrasted with the conditions in the camps of the Western Allies, the Soviet Special Camps were catastrophic. The Soviets simply used former concentration camps for their purposes, including Buchenwald and Sachsenhausen. At times, Jewish people and Communists were incarcerated, who had just survived the Nazi concentration camps. Only a tiny portion of the 130,000 German pris-

replace those German prisoners of war already there who had meanwhile become incapacitated for work. Of the 80,000 men however, only 5,000 were in good enough shape for the years of hard labor. Overall, 40,000 people died in Soviet Special Camps, of tuberculosis, typhoid, dysentery, above all however from malnutrition. 786 were executed at gunpoint. During the spring of 1950, the Soviet Union dissolved the last of the three camps. The remaining prisoners were either convicted by expedited procedures ("Waldheimer Prozesse") or dismissed. Until the Wall came down, the existence of the Special Camps had been a political taboo in the GDR.

29 Secretly taken photograph of the Special Camp at Sachsenhausen

25
Steinstuecken Exclave
⌂ 1961–1989 → Stahnsdorfer Str.,
Bernhard-Beyer-Str., Steinstr., Rot-Kreuz-
Str., Map A4 During the Cold War, the
tiny colony of Steinstuecken repeatedly
became the field on which the USA and
the Soviet Union tossed the ball back
and forth. Since 1920, the municipality
has been part of the district of Berlin-
Zehlendorf, but lay outside the city's
confines as a suburban region. In reaction to the GDR's attempt to appropriate
and forcibly integrate the exclave in
1951, the Americans symbolically stationed three US soldiers in Steinstuecken in
1952. The construction of the Wall led to
almost total isolation of the municipality,
which was the reason for the US Air
Force to keep a helicopter ready for pro-
visioning as needed. From 1972 on, after
an exchange of territory between West
Berlin and the GDR, a 100-m-wide and
1.2-km-long path connected the exclave
with the West, which then was provided
with water, electricity, and bus transportation from West Berlin.

26
Quartier Napoléon/Julius Leber
Military Barracks
⌂ Construction Council in Chief Schneidt,
1939 → Kurt-Schumacher-Damm 41,
Map B3 Ⓤ Kurt-Schumacher-Platz
France was only embraced as a victorious power in February 1945, through the
personal initiative of Winston Churchill.
In Berlin, Reinickendorf and Wedding
became part of the French occupation
zone. From August 1945, their troops were
stationed in the former military quarters of Hermann Goering, now renamed
Quartier Napoléon. In "Cités", apartment
housing for army dependents, the French
lived in a self-contained world with their
own schools, sports facilities, stores and
movie theaters. The biggest district was
the "Cité Foch" for officers, in Waid-
mannslust. The northern part of Tegel
Airport also served the French military.
Today, the jets for German government's
flight service take off from here. The
District Napoléon now serves the German
military as Julius Leber military barracks.

27
Soviet Army Nuclear Weapon
Bases Fuerstenberg and
Vogelsang
⌂ 1959 → Fürstenberg/Havel, Vogelsang, Map B1 In January 1959, the
West-German foreign intelligence service
(BND – Bundesnachrichtendienst) received alarming information through a mole
in the GDR. According to his observations
along the train track Lychen-Fuerstenberg,
80 km north of Berlin, Soviet soldiers
with heavy transporter routing equipment
seemed to have unloaded "very big
bombs". Two years prior to the Cuba
crisis, this agent thus witnessed the
extremely closely guarded stationing
of Soviet nuclear weapons on GDR
territory. From the Brandenburg bases
in Fuerstenberg and Vogelsang, the
medium-distance rockets of the Type
R-5M (Nato Code SS-3) were able to
reach cities such as London, Paris, or the
major Atlantic ports and US bases in
Western Europe. After air reconnaissance
of these attack bases by Western intelligence, the nuclear rockets were recalled
to Soviet territory in September 1959.
The former, hermetically sealed rocket
shelters and military quarters in
Fuerstenberg and Vogelsang are today
abandoned and overgrown by wild
bushes.

Plakat "We demand expiation," 1949.
"Soviet concentration camps on German
soil 1945–1950"

29 Museum about the Soviet Special Camp at Sachsenhausen

28
Hubertusstock Hunting Palace
⌂ 1848, 1973 → Hubertusstock 1, Joachimsthal, Map B1 The royal hunting lodge was built in 1848. It owed its name of palace mainly to its representative function on the occasion of major hunts. These did not stop after the end of the monarchy. But it was not sufficiently luxurious for Hermann Goering, and he constructed "Carinhall" with its pompous facilities. After the war, the grounds served as a health retreat for police officers until 1971, when the deteriorated building had to be demolished for safety reasons. The renovated Hunting Palace served the GDR government thereafter as a guesthouse. The West-German chancellor Helmut Schmidt resided here during his visit in 1981, later also the Bavarian premier Franz Josef Strauss.

29
Soviet Special Camp/ Memorial Site Sachsenhausen Concentration Camp
⌂ 1936 → Str. der Nationen 22, Oranienburg, Map B1 ⊙ Tue–Sun 8.30–18 As a model for camps and for training of the SS and as a concentration camp in the immediate vicinity of the Reich capital, Sachsenhausen had a special place in the camp system of the Nazis. In 1938, the administration of all concentration camps in the German sphere of power was centralized at Sachsenhausen.

Until 1945, more than 200,000 people were incarcerated here. Tens of thousands were killed by hunger, disease, forced labor, and cruel treatment, or as victims of the systematic annihilations practiced by the SS. About 3,000 persons remaining in the camp, among them patients, medical doctors and nursing staff, were freed on 22 April 1945 by Soviet and Polish units.

Only four months later, the former concentration camp grounds again became a place of horror and suffering. In August 1945, the Soviet intelligence service NKWD erected the biggest of its ten ▷ **Soviet Special Camps** here. The perpetrators among the Germans were to be punished here, but mainly young followers of the Nazis were caught, the small men of the Nazi party, and many innocent civilians. In the stone barracks of "Zone II", preserved until today, former Soviet forced laborers were also detained here, who had just survived the Nazis' concentra-tion camps. The NKWD treated them like traitors and had them deported to Siberian camps.

The camp was closed down in March 1950. About 8,000 prisoners were released. 5,500 were transferred to GDR prisons. Until then, 60,000 people had passed through Sachsenhausen. 12,000 people died from the gruesome conditions of incarceration or from hunger and disease. Among the dead, who were ditched in mass graves around the camp without clothes and without identification, were

33 Rumanian mountain landscape and plastic geraniums in the former shelter canteen

also prominent persons like the actor Heinrich George, who had become famous during the "Third Reich". In 1961, the GDR erected a memorial site in Sachsenhausen. Almost exclusively the Communist victims of national socialist concentration camps are honored with memorials. The history of racism and anti-Semitism remains largely cut out and ignored. Only since the end of the GDR has this part of history been made evident again in the new memorial site.

30
Shelter of Erich Honecker and the National Defense Council of the GDR

⌂ 1988 → Ützdorfer Str. Prenden, Map D1 A few kilometers north-east of the ▷ **Forest residential area of Wandlitz,** close to the little village of Prenden, the biggest nuclear shelter of the GDR was built under the cover name "Filigran" in 1988. Three storeys into the ground, the construction was to shelter 17 members of the National Defense Council in case of war, among them Erich Honecker, and an additional 500 selected persons. In its time, the site was one of the most modern and technically advanced shelters. The most important rooms swing freely, hanging attached to 6.8-cm-thick steel ropes. Additionally, fenders were to decrease the effect of the pressure wave from a nearby nuclear explosion. Similar to the former government shelter of West

Germany in the Ahr valley near Bonn (cover name "Service Site Mariental"), this shelter at Prenden today stands unused and sealed off.

31
Forest Residential Area Wandlitz / Brandenburg Clinic

⌂ 1960 → Brandenburgallee 1, Bernau, Map C1 After the people's uprisings on 17 June 1953 in the GDR and in 1956 in Hungry it was considered necessary to transfer the highest leadership quarters of the SED to a strongly protected area on the outskirts of East Berlin. The region of Wandlitz, about 40 kilometers north of Berlin, offered the best conditions. Far away from the "working class", about 23 members of the Politburo and their families resided in this forest area from 1960 – 89:

- **Otto Grotewohl** – Bussardweg 1
- **Egon Krenz** – Bussardweg 4
- **Willi Stoph** – Bussardweg 6
- **Walter Ulbricht** – Habichtweg 1
- **Erich Honecker** – Habichtweg 5
- **Erich Mielke** – Eichelhaeherweg 1
- **Guenter Schabowski** – Eichelhaeherweg 6

A 2-m-high Wall surrounded the "inner ring" of the forest area, secured by the ▷ **Ministry of State Security** "Felix E. Dzierzynski Guard Regiment". Behind the protection lines, no desire of these administrators was to remain unmet. There was a club house, a supermarket for the more exquisite socialist needs, and

Erich Honecker 1912–1994

Erich Honecker was the son of a miner in Neunkirchen, Saarland. After joining the KPD and training at the "Lenin School" in Moscow, he worked for the communist underground in Berlin. The Gestapo arrested him for his activities in 1935 and incarcerated him in a high-security prison in Brandenburg-Goerden until 1945. After the war he joined the KPD around Walter Ulbricht and was co-founder and head of the Free German Youth (FDJ – Freie Deutsche Jugend). From 1946, Honecker was part of the party leadership of the SED and advanced, as Secretary of the Central Committee for Matters of Security and Personnel, to the most important man behind Ulbricht, in 1958. He was largely responsible for the construction of the Wall and defended it as an **"antifascist protection line"**. In 1971, Honecker replaced Ulbricht as First Secretary of the Central Committee of the SED and was also head of the State Council as well as of the National Defense Council from 1976. As a result of the radical political transformations in the GDR, he had to step down in 1989. The courts thereafter investigated Honecker's misuse of power in office, high treason, and the order to shoot on the inner-German border. In 1992, the investigations against Honecker were ended for reasons of his health. In 1994 he died of liver cancer in Santiago de Chile.

Wandlitz
Kreis Bernau
Bez. Frankfurt/O.

even imports from the West presented no problem. Erich Honecker was prone to a private feudal hobby despite his presumed modesty. In the nearby Schorfheide, where Hermann Goering enjoyed hunting before him, Honecker shot up to 12 deer per day. For means of transportation, he drove a Range Rover and a Mercedes Benz. Of all historical periods, it was when the GDR was already approaching its end and thousands of people sought refuge in the West-German embassy in Prague, that Honecker is reported to have shot the biggest deer ever seen in the Schorfheide. Today, convalescent guests of the Brandenburg Clinic reside in the houses of the elite of the former GDR leadership. The main gate is preserved but yields freely to the expansive area. Guided tours and information material are available.

32
Wilhelm Pieck College

Schweitzer, H. C. Bartels, 1939. Hermann Henselmann, Kurt Liebknecht 1951–1955 → Lanke am Bogensee, Map D1 The "Waldhof" on Bogensee lake, about 40 kilometers north of Berlin, was a royally magnificent country house for Hitler's Minister of Propaganda Joseph Goebbels from 1939 on. The Red Army took over this manor house in April 1945, which was left totally unscathed by the war.

On 22 May 1946, the "Waldhof" hosted the inauguration of the first training seminar of the Central College of the Free German Youth. The training was then still under control of the Allies. From 1951 on, a monumental castle-like facility came into existence here, turning the college into a communist "cadre training unit". Strictly guarded from the public, the pupils were to receive a Marxist-Leninist basic education in one-year training seminars to qualify for activities as administrators in the FDJ. Its dogmatic training conditions soon earned the college on Bogensee the label "Red Monastery". Until the Wall came down, more than 15,000 students graduated from this school. After temporary use by various educational sponsors, the premises

Wandlitz and the "Red Monastery"

have been standing empty since 1999. The city of Berlin is currently seeking a buyer for the 150,000-square-meter area.

33
Shelter for the GDR Minister of National Defense

⌂ 1976 → Lindenallee 1, Harnekop, Map D3 ⏲ March till October Sat–Sun 10–16, November till February Sat–Sun 12–14 North-east of Berlin, between Strausberg and Bad Freienwalde, stands the small unpretentious village of Harnekop. An uneven road made of concrete tiles leads deep into the forest to object 16/102, one of the most secret buildings of the GDR. It is the shelter for the Minister of National Defense. Its construction in 1976 was achieved under highest secrecy, 30 m deep into the local sandy ground. After a nuclear attack, the East German army (NVA) was to operate from here. 455 men (women were prohibited from entering) could have survived up to a month in this hermetically sealed fortress. The 3-m-thick walls and the 7-m-strong ceiling would have resisted a nuclear bomb 200 times as strong as the Hiroshima bomb. The interior has kilometers of hallways, which

Hunting trophy shot by Honecker at Schorfheide near Wandlitz

lead to about 150 chambers for shelter for the command and the general recreation areas. This facility is preserved until today close to its typical 1970s original GDR design. A photograph of a Rumanian mountain landscape decorates the concrete wall of the canteen. On a table in front of it stand pink and red plastic geraniums. Until 1993, the German military ran the shelter. Today it is open to visitors as an underground relic of the Cold War.

31 Gate to the former forest residential area Wandlitz, residential area for top SED party members

31 Walter Ulbricht's former private home at Wandlitz

32 Former "Wilhelm Pieck College"

Glossary

Bundeswehr – armed forces of the Federal Republic of Germany

FRG (Federal Republic of Germany) – official name for West Germany (German: BRD)

Gauleiter – high-ranking Nazi official, appointed by Hitler and responsible for a particular region in Germany; later also in Austria and Czechoslovakia

GDR (German Democratic Republic) – official name for East Germany, (German: DDR)

KPD (Kommunistische Partei Deutschlands) – German Communist Party

KZ (Konzentrationslager) – concentration camp

Leibstandarte SS – SS unit specifically charged with the protection of the "Fuehrer"

Nazi – abbreviation for National Socialists

NSDAP (National Socialist German Workers' Party) – Official name of the Nazi party

NVA (Nationale Volksarmee) – army of the GDR

Oberkommando – Supreme Command

Plattenbau – building made of prefabricated concrete slabs, often found in central and eastern Europe. The word is a compound of Platte (slab) and Bau (building)

SED (Sozialistische Einheitspartei) – Socialist Unity Party of the GDR

StaeV (Staendige Vertretung) – Permanent Representation of the FRG government in the GDR

Stasi (Staatssicherheit) – official security arm of the GDR government

ZK (Zentralkomitee) – Central Committee

Select Bibliography

Delius, Friedrich Christian; Lapp, Peter Joachim: Transit Westberlin. Erlebnisse im Zwischenraum, Berlin 2000.

Demps, Laurenz: Berlin-Wilhelmstraße. Eine Topographie preußisch-deutscher Macht, Berlin 2000.

Etzold, Alfred; Türk, Wolfgang: Der Dorotheenstädtische Friedhof. Die Begräbnisstätten an der Berliner Chausseestraße, Berlin 2002.

Haubrich, Rainer; Hoffmann, Hans Wolfgang; Meuser, Philipp: Berlin. Der Architekturführer. Berlin 2001.

Holper, Anne; Käther, Matthias: DDR-Baudenkmale in Berlin – Berlins Osten neu entdeckt. Berlin 2003.

Isaacs, Jeremy; Downing, Taylor: Der Kalte Krieg. München 2001.

Jander, Martin: Berlin (DDR). Ein politischer Spaziergang, Berlin 2003.

Kleihues, Josef P.; Becker-Schwering, Jan G.; Kahlfeldt, Paul (Hg.): Bauen in Berlin 1900–2000. Berlin 2000.

Kowalczuk, Ilko-Sascha; Wolle, Stefan: Roter Stern über Deutschland. Berlin 2001.

Oswalt, Philipp: Berlin – Stadt ohne Form. Strategien einer anderen Architektur, München 2000.

Presse- und Informationsamt des Landes Berlin (Hg.): Berlin-Handbuch. Das Lexikon der Bundeshauptstadt, Berlin 1992.

Ritter, Jürgen; Lapp, Peter Joachim: Die Grenze. Ein deutsches Bauwerk, Berlin 2001.

Schulze, Hans M.: In den Villen der Agenten. Die Stasi-Prominenz privat, Berlin 2003.

Stiftung Haus der Geschichte der BRD (Hg.): Erlebnis Geschichte. Geschichte vom Zweiten Weltkrieg bis heute. Katalog zur Ausstellung, Bergisch Gladbach 2003.

Wetzlaugk, Udo: Die Alliierten in Berlin. Berlin 1988.

Wörner, Martin; Mollenschott, Doris; Hüter, Karl H.; Siegel, Paul: Architekturführer Berlin. Berlin 2001

Photographs

Imprint

A catalogue record for this publication is available from the Deutsche Bibliothek in the Deutsche Nationalbibliographie; detailed bibliographical data are available on the internet at http://dnb.ddb.de

First english edition, September 2006
© Christoph Links Verlag –
LinksDruck GmbH, 2005
Schönhauser Allee 36
10435 Berlin
Tel.: (030) 44 02 32-0
www.linksverlag.de
mail@linksverlag.de

Front cover design: Maik Kopleck

Text/Design/Illustrations/Maps, DTP:
Maik Kopleck, STAAB/KOPLECK:DESIGN!
www.staab-kopleck-design.de

Translation from German: Irene Grote

Printed by:
AZ Druck und Datentechnik, Kempten

ISBN-10:   3-86153-411-8
ISBN-13: 978-3-86153-411-2

Maik Kopleck
Born in 1975, studied Communication Design at the University of Applied Sciences in Düsseldorf, was a freelance Art Director with several advertising agencies in Düsseldorf and Berlin. During longer stays in the USA, he worked as a freelance photographer in San Francisco and is now co-director of the design company STAAB/KOPLECK:DESIGN! in Düsseldorf, founded in 1996. The first publication in the Past Finder Series of city guides was the "PastFinder® Berlin 1933–45" in 2004.

In Zusammenarbeit mit der
STIFTUNG
AUFARBEITUNG

FURTHER TITLES IN THE PAST FINDER SERIES:

PAST FINDER **BERLIN** 1933-1945
3rd edition
ISBN 978-3-86153-326-X

PAST FINDER **OBERSALZBERG** 1933-1945
1st edition
ISBN 978-3-86153-355-3

PAST FINDER **MÜNCHEN** 1933-1945
2nd edition
ISBN 978-3-86153-354-5

PAST FINDER **BERLIN** 1933-1945
English Edition
ISBN 978-3-86153-363-4

PAST FINDER **MUNICH** 1933-1945
English Edition
ISBN 978-3-86153-410-X

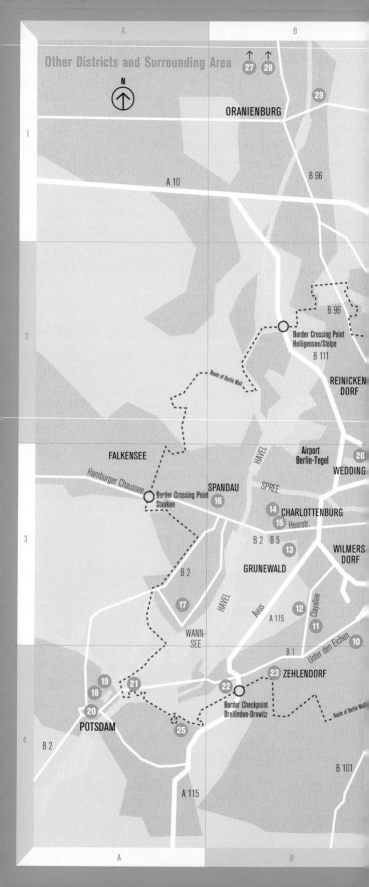

Other Districts and Surrounding Area

N

ORANIENBURG

A 10

B 96

Border Crossing Point
Heiligensee/Stolpe

B 96

B 111

REINICKEN
DORF

FALKENSEE

Hamburger Chaussee

Border Crossing Point
Staaken

SPANDAU

Route of Berlin Wall

HAVEL

SPREE

Airport
Berlin-Tegel

WEDDING

CHARLOTTENBURG

Heerstr.

B 2 B 5

GRUNEWALD

B 2

HAVEL

WILMERS
DORF

Avus

A 115

Clayallee

WANN-
SEE

B 1

Unter den Eichen

POTSDAM

B 2

A 115

ZEHLENDORF

Border Checkpoint
Dreilinden-Drewitz

Route of Berlin Wall

B 101